CW01494951

LISBON

Vitor Manuel Adrião

JONGLEZ PUBLISHING

Travel guides

Born in Lisbon in 1959, **Vitor Manuel Adrião** has a degree in history and philosophy, and is an acknowledged specialist in the history of Lisbon and Portugal. The author of *The Secret History of Portugal*, he is also a specialist in the country's esoteric traditions. A lecturer and essayist, he is the author of more than 40 books.

Secret Lisbon is a new type of guidebook. Its author, Vitor Manuel Adrião, has brought to light the very unique character of this city which, according to some, is destined to become the spiritual capital of Europe.

This guidebook has thus been adapted to the city and, contrary to our other publications, contains numerous esoteric elements, making it a veritable guide of initiation.

We have made a considerable effort to ensure that this information remains accessible for readers who are unfamiliar with this tradition. We have also tried to clarify things by adding several themed passages whose purpose is to provide the keys to understanding these topics which are too often impenetrable for the general public.

Like our other guides, *Secret Lisbon* also includes places, people and anecdotes that we hope will allow you to continue to discover the unusual, secret or unknown aspects of this capital city.

Secret Lisbon also sheds light on the numerous yet overlooked details of places we pass by every day.

These details invite us to pay more attention to our urban landscape and, more generally, to regard our city with the same curiosity and attention we often have when traveling.

Comments about the guidebook and its contents, as well as information on sites we haven't mentioned, are welcome. Your comments will help us enrich our future editions.

Please contact us at:
E-mail: info@jonglezpublishing.com

CONTENTS

Alfama, Graça, Mouraria

Baixa, Rossio

Bairro Alto, Santa Catarina, Chiado, Campo Santana

Lapa, Madragoa, Estrela, Campo de Ourique

CONTENTS

Belém, Santo Amaro, Ajuda

Farther away

Alfama, Graça, Mouraria

VILA BERTA

Revival of a forgotten workers' village

Rua da Vila Berta à Graça
(between Beco do Forno do Sol and Travessa da Pereira)
Tram 28E – Funicular da Graça

At the end of the 19th century, Lisbon's population expanded dramatically, largely due to the massive influx of rural Portuguese in search of work in the city. In order to cope with this, new working-class districts grew up and, with them, new forms of housing known as *vilas operárias*, typically making the most of the limited space. Vila Berta, with around 30 of these houses, is one of a few thousand 'workers' villages' constructed in Lisbon. From an architectural point of view, this is considered the most interesting of the surviving streets.

Built between 1902 and 1908 by Joaquim Francisco Tojal, a property developer in the Graça district keen to make a profitable investment, Vila Berta consists of two rows of houses with pale yellow facades divided by an alleyway. On the west side, three-storey buildings are separated by small gardens. They are remarkable for their raised terraces with wrought-iron balustrades supported by pillars. On the east side, the houses have only two floors and simple balconies. The architectural references of Vila Berta, named after the developer's daughter, are multiple. The azulejo frieze bearing the name is influenced by Art Nouveau, while the wrought iron evokes European turn-of-the-century architecture.

Vila Berta wasn't always such a charming and colourful place. A few years ago, time had taken its toll on the housing and it was very run down. The rock-bottom rents meant that owners had no incentive to carry out any work to halt this slow decline. In 2015, however, the Vila Berta renovation project was launched by architect Joana Grilo of the Vai association, thanks to funding from Lisbon City Council. The intervention of this architect, together with local residents, gained wide support both among the Portuguese public and from private companies (including Energias de Portugal, Portugal Telecom and Weber International), which finally helped to revive the fortunes of Vila Berta.

THE STARS
OF ESTRELA D'OURO

A 'Masonic' district

Graça district
Visits sometimes allowed on request
Tram 12E, 28E

Located between No. 22 rua da Graça (Grace street) and No. 14 rua da Senhora do Monte (Our Lady of the Mount street), the Estrela d'Ouro (Golden Star) district was designed in 1907 by the architect Manuel Joaquim Norte Júnior. It was built in 1908 on the initiative of Agapito Serra Fernandes, a Galician confectionery manufacturer, to house his workers. Completed in 1909, this 'villa', as working-class neighbourhoods used to be called, consisted of 120 households organised into small two- or three-floored buildings built around the Rosalina residence (the owner's home) which stood, isolated, in the centre. Now a retirement home, it is located at No. 13 Josefa Maria street. The gate, which is often left open, leads to a charming collection of homes and gardens, including a beautiful vegetable garden to the left.

In an astonishing manner, this neighbourhood is dotted with five-pointed stars. They are on the pavements, the fronts of buildings, everywhere! An important Freemasonry symbol, this star is a reminder of Agapito Serra Fernandes' Masonic membership. He was probably a member of the 'Estrella del Noroeste' (Northwest Star) Lodge founded in 1880 in Betanzos (in Galicia's A Coruña province), which was loyal to the United Grand Orient of Lusitania. It is a known fact that architect

Norte Júnior was a Grand Orient of Lusitania Freemason who practiced the ancient and accepted Scottish Rite. He even held an important role in the 'Amor da Pátria' (Love for the Homeland) Masonic Lodge in Horta, on the Azores archipelago. The layout of the Estrela d'Ouro district is U-shaped and the streets and squares bear the names of members of Agapito Fernandes' family. Take note of the pretty polychrome azulejo panels showing the owner's name, with the star illustrating the district's name (it is sometimes sculpted in relief).

The *Ciné Royal* used to be located in this neighbourhood. Inaugurated at the end of 1929, it was the first cinema in Portugal to project films with sound. On 5 April 1930, *White Shadows in the South Seas*, MGM's first film, directed by Van Dyke (who also did the sound), was shown in the presence of the president of the Republic. Now a supermarket (No. 100 rua da Graça), the former cinema's pretty period clock has been preserved.

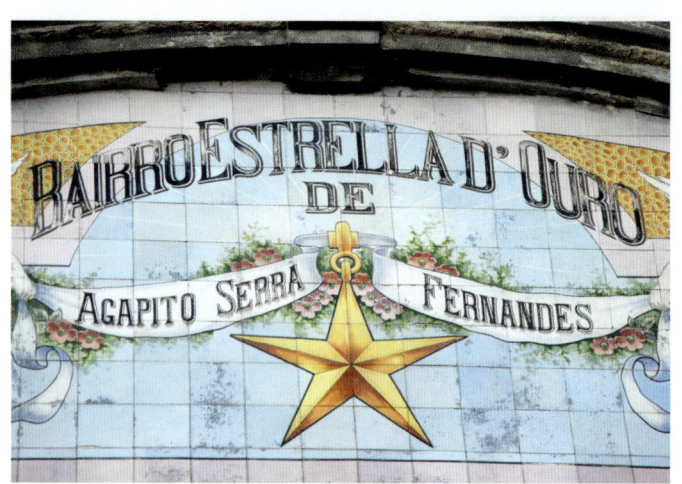

BAIRRO ESTRELLA D'OURO
DE
AGAPITO SERRA FERNANDES

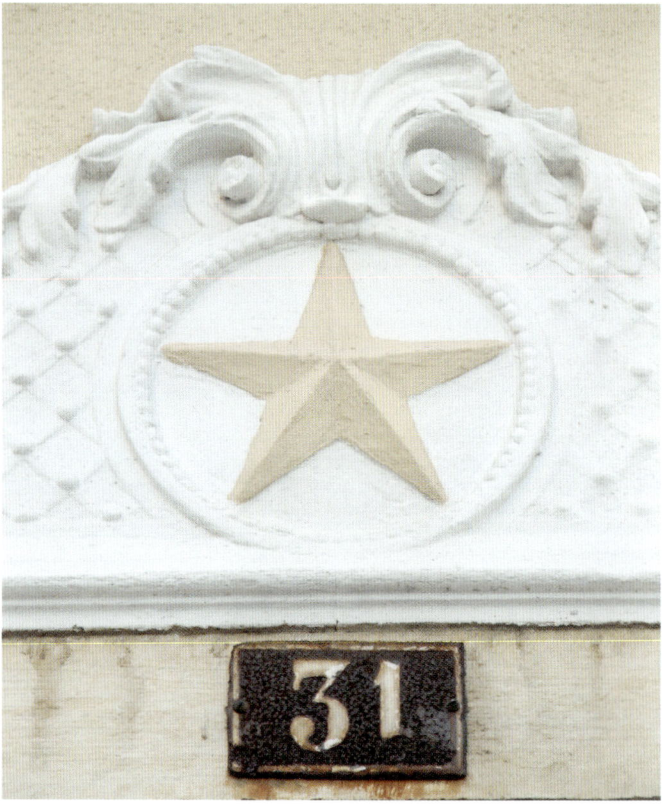
31

SAINT GEN'S CHAIR

Have a seat for a happy childbirth

Nossa Senhora do Monte and São Gens chapel
Senhora do Monte Belvedere
Wednesday to Sunday, 10am–noon and 4pm–8pm
Tram 12E, 28E

The Nossa Senhora do Monte and São Gens chapel is the site of a rather curious tradition. Behind the entrance, in a small cell hidden from the public by a wooden door, is the famous Saint Gens' chair (*trono do Santo Jina*), a marble monolith polished into an ergonomic shape by time and the pregnant women who used it.

The legendary character São Gens was, it seems, the seventh Christian bishop of Olisipo (Roman Lisbon), soon after AD 300. He was also the disciple of one of the Iberian apostles of Saint James Major, who arrived in the Spanish territory shortly after Christ's Crucifixion.

It is said that his mother died giving birth to him. This legend is the origin of a curious tradition in which the pregnant women of Lisbon, hoping for a happy childbirth, come to sit on 'Saint Gens' chair'. Once located outside the chapel, it is now kept inside. Ordinary women kept alive a tradition that was followed by several queens of Portugal, such as Catarina (Catherine of Castile), Dom João III's wife and Dom Sebastião's grandmother, who sat on the miraculous 'chair'.

Four Augustinian hermit monks founded this chapel once Afonso Henriques had taken Lisbon from the Moors. At the beginning of the 13th century, improvements were made by Dona Susana, a noblewoman, as a show of gratitude for her happy childbirth, a fact that contributed to the site's miraculous reputation. It was at this time that the chapel was dedicated to Nossa Senhora da Visitação do Monte.

Saint Gens owes his name to the contraction of the Latin *genesius* or *genésio*, meaning genesis. The use of the marble chair is thus in perfect accord with the saint's name.

TÁVORA PALACE

A charming spectacle

Travessa da Nazaré, 21, Mouraria
Daily, 2pm–10.30pm (free)
Fado nights announced at: radioonline.com.pt/amalia

Now occupied by the Mouraria Sports Club, the 18th-century Távora Palace is one of Lisbon's most remarkable and least well-known palaces. Its former stables are now used as a gymnasium and the old kitchen is still decorated with its azulejos, known as *padrão*, which date from the Pombaline era (second half of the 18th century) and cover it completely.

In the wake of the earthquake that destroyed Lisbon in 1755, during the ministry of the Marquis of Pombal, Prime Minister to King Joseph [José] I, the need arose for an inexpensive and easy-to-produce covering material. The ceramic factories were engaged in the large-scale production of *padrão* azulejos for the brand-new residential buildings: these azulejos could be combined in an infinite variety of styles.

The former main hall of the palace, known today as the 'Cathedral of Fado', is delightful, with its 18th-century paintings decorating the wooden ceiling and walls. Surrounded by cherubs and roses, a picture of Prudentia adorns the entrance to the hall.

She is personified by two figures, who display her trappings, the mirror and the serpent. Looking in the mirror is an expression of self-knowledge, since no one is able to master their actions without knowing themselves and being able to correct their faults. The reptile, symbol of ancient wisdom represented in the Greek goddess Athena, protects its head when attacked by coiling around itself: this acts as a moral lesson that one must do everything to defend oneself against evil. Hence, the Bible teaches that we are to be 'as shrewd as serpents and innocent as doves' (Matthew 10:16).

This prudence was not sufficient to protect the Távora family from the fury, persecution and extermination inflicted on them by the Marquis of Pombal, who accused them of opposing King Joseph – an accusation based solely on the self-interest of the marquis, and which remains unproven to this day.

The Távora Palace also had a hall decorated with 19th-century frescoes, which included images of the Pena Palace in Sintra, but they have been erased as part of a mysterious scheme hatched by the city council, the current owners of the building.

COLÉGIO DOS MENINOS ÓRFÃOS ⑤

A veritable marvel of Portuguese azulejo art

Rua da Mouraria, 64
Generally closed to the public
Entry is sometimes possible by politely asking at the entrance
Metro Martim Moniz

Behind the Mouraria shopping centre, at No. 64 Mouraria street, is the entrance to the *Colégio dos Meninos Órfãos* (School for Orphaned Boys), which is under the invocation of Our Lady of Montserrat.

As the door is usually left open, the visit has a certain 'semi-forbidden' character that gives it a kind of charm. After crossing a small patio and passing through a majestic Rococo-style gate (from the Dom João V period), you arrive before a veritable marvel of Portuguese azulejo art – a set of 18th-century panels in Rococo frames that stretch all the way up the four floors of the building's staircase. The only one of its kind in Lisbon, it depicts the entire history of the Virgin Mary's ancestors from the House of David, up to the announcement of the Passion of Christ, when as a boy Jesus disappeared from his mother's house and she found him in the Temple among the high priests. This azulejo piece symbolises the former function of the Orphanage School, which was to provide a home to these fatherless and motherless children who were left on their own. They often lived in gangs and roamed aimlessly through Lisbon's streets.

Queen Dona Beatrice, the wife of Dom Afonso III (Dom Dinis' father), had this home for abandoned children built in 1273. Queen Dona Catherine, the wife of Dom João III, had it renovated in 1549 to welcome more than 30 orphans. She placed it into the good hands of the Society of Jesus, making it the oldest Jesuit orphanage school in the world and transforming it into a unique educational establishment. The building was renovated yet again in 1745 at the request of Dom José I.

After the abolition of the religious orders in 1834, the Colégio dos Meninos Órfãos declined, eventually losing its original function. In the mid-20th century, the building was transformed into a police station (which was later transferred elsewhere), and then into a gym. Conservation work on the building was carried out in 1989 and 1990.

THE CURIOSITIES OF MENINO DEUS CHURCH

When Baby Jesus gave Dom João V an heir

Igreja do Menino Deus
Calçada do Menino Deus, 15–27
Visits on reservation through the Patriarchate of Lisbon at 218 810 500
Tram 12E, 28E

Spared by the earthquake of 1755, the astonishing *Igreja do Menino Deus* (Church of the Child God) can only be visited by reservation. At the beginning of the 18th century, a few homes and a chapel that the religious members of São Francisco de Xabregas' Ordem Terceira had acquired to found a hospital stood on this spot. A nun from the *Madre de Deus* (Mother of God) convent offered this new religious edifice a small statue of Baby Jesus. Believed to be miraculous, it was immediately named *Menino Deus* and still exists today.

This name was later extended to the monks' hospital as well as to the new church donated by Dom João V, who had made a vow regarding the long-awaited birth of his first heir. His child's arrival was attributed to the intervention of *Menino Deus* who thus expressed his desire to perpetuate the Lusitanian monarchy, a lineage considered divine ever since Christ had miraculously appeared to Dom Afonso Henriques at Ourique.

Thus, on 4 July 1711, in the presence of the royal family and court, the king laid the first stone of this new church, inaugurating a series of royal building projects that would culminate in the magnificent Mafra convent, the most symbolic Joanina (Rococo style under Dom João V) construction.

The design of this church is attributed to architect João Antunes, and it was his last accomplishment. His plan is original. With the deep apse and unique rectangular nave with cut-off corners, he created a unified, non-centralised space and the illusion of an enveloping shroud that is accentuated by the arrangement of the lecterns.

The *Igreja do Menino Deus*, whose Mannerist-style facade integrates Baroque elements, is considered to be an architectural model for later Baroque churches whose inspired style strives to humanise the divine, just as Gothicism had earlier deified humanity. Thus, this church inaugurated a new set of ideas for architecture and art, as illustrated in its interior decor, a veritable artistic sampling of Joanina style.

THE CISTERN OF SAINT MICHAEL OF ALFAMA ⑦

Alfama-the-good-waters

Museu do Fado – Largo do Chafariz de Dentro, Alfama – 218 823 470
Tuesday to Sunday, 10am–6pm
Guided tour of the cistern by appointment
Metro Santa Apolónia

The waters of *Alfama* or *Águas Orientais* (Oriental waters) were introduced into Lisbon's water distribution system in 1868 through the construction of a cistern and pumping station to replace the former *Chafariz da Praia* (Beach Fountain). The cistern held the water while the steam pumping station propelled it up to the recently constructed Verónica water tower (1862). The *Museu do Fado* (Fado Museum) is located in this cistern, which can be visited by appointment. The water pumping station's steam machinery has also been preserved in what is now the Fado Museum's auditorium. The enormous cistern is in the courtyard. To access it, you descend a staircase that leads to an underground gallery of arches where the water runs in pipes towards this urban reservoir that was the main water distribution centre for the neighbourhoods around Alfama until the early 1950s. At the end of the 19th century, these waters, whose temperature sometimes exceeds 20 °C, were classed as mineral and medicinal waters. From the 17th century, they were used for the public baths (*alcaçarias*) that remained in use up to the beginning of the 20th century. The use of these thermal waters for therapeutic reasons was recognised in the 17th century. Of the two springs that fed the *Alcaçarias*

do Duque, for example, the first served to treat skin diseases, digestive problems and allergies, while the second was used for rheumatism, respiratory ailments and women's health problems. Alfama's main public baths were the *Alcaçarias do Duque* (water temperatures of 30–34 °C), the *Banhos de Dona Clara* (24–28 °C), the *Alcaçarias do Baptista* (32–34 °C) located near São João da Praça at the end of rua do Barão, and the *Banhos do Doutor* (27 °C). After work on the pipes, the spring that used to supply Alfama's *Tanque das Lavadeiras* (Washerwomen's Wash-House) was uncovered. The supposed healing properties of these waters were so reputed that people came from all parts of the country to test them. The waters, which contain chloride and sulphur but have a low salt content, rise to the surface through a geological fault in the Miocene layers, a fact that you can check on Lisbon Council's geological map. The *Alcaçarias* group structurally originates from five faults roughly oriented north-east to south-west.

Why does the El Rei fountain have six water outlets?

On the corner of Rua Cais de Santarém and Largo do Terreiro do Trigo, the El Rei Fountain (*Chafariz d'El Rei*) used to have as many as nine water outlets. Today there are only six remaining, each with its own specific function. Following a decree issued on 30 June 1542, the fountain became the only water supply point for the entire city and drew huge crowds of people. Exasperated by the often unbearable queues to use the taps, users began to argue or even fight with one another. A city by-law issued in 1551 put an end to these disputes by allocating a different water outlet to each social class. The most easterly was reserved for non-white and mixed-race men; the second for galley slaves; the third and fourth for white women and white men respectively; the fifth for non-white and mixed-race women; and the sixth for white servants. Those who failed to respect this order were required to pay a fine to the city, set according to their financial means. A plaque fixed to the right-hand wall records the successive renovations carried out on the fountain. Erected c. 1220 during the reign of Afonso II, the fountain was moved inside

the Fernandina Wall by King Denis in 1308. In order to thank their ruler for this practical initiative, the people renamed it the Fountain of the King. Remodelled by successive kings, and damaged by the earthquake of 1755, it owes its present appearance to the last restructuring work undertaken in 1864.

THE SYMBOLS
OF SAINT LUCIA

Divine wisdom at Saint Lucia of Malta church

Santa Luzia de Malta Church
Largo de Santa Luzia
Daily, 10am–6pm
Tram 12E, 28E

Rebuilt after the earthquake of 1755, *Santa Luzia de Malta* (Saint Lucia of Malta) church bears an azulejo portrait of Saint Lucia on its lateral facade, in addition to two other large azulejo panels representing the conquest of Lisbon and the praça do Comércio before

the earthquake. Made in the *Fábrica da Viúva Lamego*, they are the work of artist António Quaresma.

Most of the statues once located inside the church have been transferred to the neighbouring São Tiago church, but a few contemporary images of the Order of Malta and the tombs of several noble knights can still be admired.

Many Christian saints are iconographic adaptations of Celtic, Greek and Roman gods for whom Christianity forged sacred legends, thus attributing them with a human existence. Nevertheless, these are fictional stories that only obtain their strength and meaning from the devotion of the people.

Luzia is thus the Christianised equivalent of Lusina (*luzia*, *luz* ...), the Celt-Iberian Sun goddess. She has been kept near the *portas do Sol* (Sun doors) out of respect for the archaic tradition of the sacred enclaves where this saint was, or still is, worshipped.

No study of the martyrs recounts the torture of Saint Lucia, yet it is said that she had her eyes ripped out. She is often depicted carrying her eyes on a platter, thus illustrating the meaning of her name, 'she who emits light'. Her feast day, 13 December, almost the time of the winter solstice (the birth of light), portrays her as a saint who brings clarity and teaching, like the goddess Lusina, the companion of the god Lug who sent her to teach her arts to humans. Perhaps this is why the blind invoke her, as in symbolic terms seeing is equated with knowing, and blindness to ignorance.

Thus, the symbolism of *Luzia*, through the luminosity of her name and her attributes (the eyes are sometimes replaced by a lamp or candle), associates her with the ancient goddesses of Wisdom and Light.

The legend of Santa Luzia (Saint Lucia)

According to legend, Lucia, the virgin of Syracuse (13 December), took her ill mother to the tomb of Saint Agatha in Catania, and, upon her mother's recovery, distributed her belongings to the poor. Denounced to the magistrate Paschasius for being Christian, she was condemned to live in a brothel. She resisted so strongly, however, that even two pairs of yoked oxen failed to move her. She was cruelly tortured. Her eyes were ripped out and, finally, her throat was slit. She thus died a martyr in AD 304. Her attributes are symbolised by two eyes on a platter and, sometimes, by yoked oxen. The legend is thus a reminder that the integrity of the light of religious devotion, sent by God, is such that no mortal man may desecrate it.

Protection from fever or sore throats:
the miracles of Saint Blaise

Built in the shape of a Latin cross, Santa Luzia church gives the place of honour to a rare statue of Saint Blaise, a saint reported to be miraculous among Lisbon residents suffering from fevers and sore throats, as well as blind people and those who stutter.

The legend of Saint Blaise (*São Brás*), a Christian bishop martyred by the Romans in Armenia in AD 316, says that he pulled a fishbone out of a child's throat by hand before then placing two lit candles in the shape of a cross on his mouth.

This explains why he became the patron saint of throat ailments, as well as the protector of guilds for the professional manufacturers of candles and other wax-based products.

The life-size statue shows Saint Blaise in liturgical robes holding an Episcopal cross. His robe bears the cross of the Order of Malta, of which he was a patron saint (see opposite), after Saint John the Baptist, the primary protector of this military and religious institution.

According to legend, on 3 February, in the middle of winter, Saint Blaise followed a divine calling and left the city of Sebaste to find refuge in a cave of Mount Argeo, whose etymological root, *arg*, means *argentum* or *argent* (silver).

Arg is related to *garg*, or *gurg*, which is the root of the word *garganta* (throat). This explains why São Brás became associated not only with throat ailments, but also with caves, thus becoming a representative of the divinities of the profound depths of the Earth.

Saint Blaise is a winter saint whose feast day follows the Feast of the Virgin of the Candlesticks, or Candlemas, on 2 February, almost as if Blaise (*brás* or *braseiro* in Portuguese, meaning 'blaze') were the Midnight Sun who, by lighting the candles, would also illuminate the long winter night.

In this context, the night signifies the depth, obscurity, and mystery that can only be revealed through the light of the sacred candles. They illuminate this argent, the symbolic expression of the pure sacredness of the moon, feminine and intuitive, which is present in this church's *Luz de Luzia*. Saint Blaise is thus not here by chance ...

Why is Saint Blaise one of the patron saints of the Order of Malta?

Saint Blaise is the exclusive patron saint of the Order of Malta in the city of Lisbon, as the Order of Portugal was apparently founded on his feast day (3 February) during the reign of Dom Afonso Henriques (in the 12th century). Of the 23 command posts that the Order of Malta had in Portugal, Lisbon's was one of the most important, both economically and politically, so much so in fact that Brother Lucas of Santa Catarina, in his memoirs of the military order of Saint John of Malta (1734), enthusiastically describes it as a Grand Priory, which it never was. At the time, the Order's headquarters were located in the Flor da Rosa Monastery at Crato, in Alentejo. The headquarters were set up there in 1340, after leaving Belver or Leça de Bailio at Matosinhos.

THE UNUSUAL CAPITALS OF LISBON CATHEDRAL

Not just a symbol of the struggle between Christians and Muslims ...

Largo da Sé
Monday to Saturday, 10am–6pm
Tram 28E

The construction of the Sé (cathedral) of Lisbon, the work of the 12th-century master of the Builder-Monks Frei Roberto de Lisboa (see p. 55), began in Roman times and was completed in the Gothic period. Stunning Roman capitals adorn both sides of the central door of the cathedral's main entrance.

One capital shows two knights fighting, one astride a lion and the other astride a bull – a rather strange representation of the *psychomachia*, the moral struggle between Christians (the bearded knight and the lion are linked to the Light, the Sun, and Christ) and Moors (illustrated by the beardless knight and the bull, whose horns represent the crescent moon, the symbol of Muhammad). Beyond this simple allegorical interpretation, this strategic struggle is also viewed as an expression of the cosmic cycle of the Earth led by the Sun and the Moon, which illustrates the very essence of Life and Death. This astronomical/astrological character, marked by the opposition between the signs of the Lion and Bull (Taurus), also designates the presence of the mixed, or androgynous, forms of worship that were celebrated in this cathedral. One form was of a public nature (Catholicism, represented by the Lion of Judah), while the other was more secret, but also supposedly celebrated here. It is represented by the Bull, a symbol of the secret or primordial Tradition.

The Archangel Michael, represented on one of the nearby capitals, mediates the union between the Lion of Judah and the Bull of Ishmael (Islam is descended from Ishmael, whose tribe had a coat of arms featuring a bull, which is also a symbol of the occult forces of spiritual power).

In this context, the presence of Archangel Michael symbolises the union of Tradition and Religion, and, by fighting the dragon (which is associated with Muslim heresy), he is also a reminder of the fact that this now Christian cathedral was once the Islamic mosque of *Al-Usbuna* (Arab Lisbon).

Principles of sacred architecture

A well-to-do man strolling through a quarry came across a group of three workers. He asked them what they were doing. 'I'm earning a living,' the apprentice replied. 'I'm cutting stone,' the journeyman answered. The third man, the master builder, looked at the stranger with disdain and declared: 'I'm building a cathedral.'

Keepers of the hermetic notions of sacred geometry, the basis of sacred architecture, the medieval Builder-Monks constituted the first operational (or cooperative) Builders Guilds that built Europe's principal Roman and Gothic monuments, and particularly the grand cathedrals. The latter were conceived so as to reproduce the Universe, so that what is above (in Heaven) is identical to what is below (on Earth) and vice versa. Although temples are a static form of celestial movement, they are nevertheless animated by the presence of the faithful.

The design of the temple floor is a well-ordered, horizontal projection of the Universe. According to solar orientation, each cardinal direction indicates an extreme position of the seasonal and daily cycle and places the temple in a harmonised movement with Space. The temple's journey reproduces the solar year, punctuated by the facades, on a path that leads from the Shadows to the Light.

In Judaeo-Christian tradition, Autumn, or Twilight, is to the west; Winter, or Midnight, is to the north; the Dawn or Daybreak of Spring is to the east; and, finally, Summer, or Noon, is to the south. This dynamic of space is used in the liturgical calendar, as depending on the period of the ritual year some doors are opened while others are closed, following the symbolism of 'Holy Doors'. The north is the darkest part of the temple. It expresses the cold, the shadows, and the invisible world that the subterranean world, or crypt, represents. All the symbolism of the north door is consecrated to the stellar origins, or the North Star.

The east indicates the beginning of the World. It is from this direction that the Sun rises, its first ray landing on the altar. It also shows the way to Jerusalem, and more importantly, Heavenly Jerusalem (a symbol of paradise). By focusing the power of the Rising Sun, it makes it shine like Life throughout the temple.

The south marks the solar zenith, the height of Creation and its fructification. It is thus where the pulpit and the Gospel, the manifestation of the Holy Word, are placed. The west is the area of contemplation and Death, where profane and sacred meet.

The main entrance is always placed to the west so mortals can reach the immortality symbolised by the altar, to the east. The west represents Autumn, the End of Time, and the end of a planetary cycle marked by the zodiac, represented here, at the centre, by the Holy Father (who symbolises the central Sun), or by the Son surrounded by the twelve apostles.

Following the *decumanus* (east to west) and the *cardo* (north to south), there are two entrances to the temple. The main entrance is called the *Door of Time* because it indicates the Sun's path through the nave from east to west, thus starting Time in the sacred Space. The *decumanus* determines the human axis of the edifice, from birth to death, or east to west. Entering by the west door allows Time to move from Life to Death or, in other words, from the neophyte who enters the temple from the exterior, to the initiate who participates in the Primordial Origin as symbolised by the main altar to the east. A side entrance, called the *Door of Eternity*, placed in relation to the *cardo* (or north to south) is also very common. The *cardo* represents the axis of Eternity and crosses the *decumanus*, which represents Time. Thus, the Time of Eternity is located beneath the vault's keystone, the philosopher's stone or cornerstone of the temple.

As the temple is the static manifestation of the Body of God, its outline represents a human body, with its arms in the shape of a cross or along its body. Each part of the temple possesses properties that can be assimilated to the human body. The circle of the apse represents the head; the crossing of the nave and the transept symbolises the heart, or the life that beats throughout the temple. As for the west facade, it represents the feet of the Body of God, thus reproducing and summarising the principles and functions of the entire building.

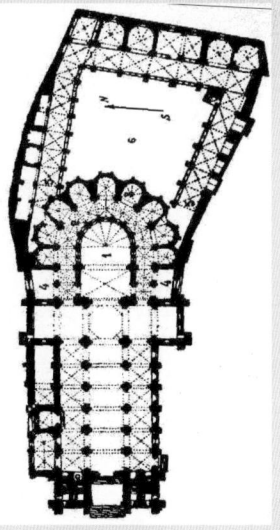

Neophytes are informed of the spiritual journey they will embark upon by reading the west facade. The 'feet' of God also evoke those of the faithful entering His Home in order to find themselves through the Grace of the Holy Spirit.

This entire arrangement creates a state of 'vibrant sympathy' between Man and the Cosmos. Entering the temple is like entering the human body, in other words an act of *introspection*. In fact, it is the execution of a principle of Judaeo-Christian tradition found in the hermetic phrase 'know yourself and you will know the Universe and the Gods'.

LISBON CATHEDRAL'S 'HOLY DOOR'

Reminder of the passage of the Holy Grail?

Largo da Sé
Monday to Saturday, 10am–6pm
Tram 28E

An earthly expression of Heaven's Gate, guarded by the Archangel Michael, the Holy Door symbolises the passage between the human realm and the realm of Heaven. Opened only on certain days fixed by the religious calendar, such as for the Jubilee, the door plays a highly important role, which is why only the most important Christian temples that strongly abide by its spiritual foundations have Holy Doors. Contrary to popular belief, it is not just the four basilicas of Rome that have Holy Doors. Upon entering Lisbon Cathedral, a discreet inscription can be seen on the left confirming the existence of a Holy Door. Outside, the other side of the door is to be found along rua do Aljube on the north

side of the building. The reasons for its existence are as rare as they are vague. The only certainty is that the door gives access to the inside of the church as well as to the Cardinal Patriarch's lodge through another small side door located in a hidden corner of the main door.

Following the creation of the Lisbon Patriarchate on 3 November 1716, the Portuguese Patriarchate esteemed that, as Saint Peter's in Rome had a Holy Door, then Lisbon Cathedral should have one as well. This claim was probably also supported by the mysterious legend according to which the Holy Grail itself (the receptacle for Christ's blood and the Virgin's tears) had supposedly passed through this door several centuries before. Taking advantage of the construction of the Patriarch's lodge in early 1717, they annexed the Holy Door, an action which attests to the Portuguese Church's desire to free itself from the politics of the Roman Church. 'The Romans have one, and so do the Portuguese', they seemed to declare.

The first Holy Door appears to have dated from the 12th century when Bishop Diego Gelmírez inaugurated the Cathedral of Santiago de Compostela's Holy Door on the occasion of the Holy Year (25 July 1101). It was not until 1499 that the Pope opened a Holy Door in Rome, most certainly inspired by the other one in Jerusalem. This door, more commonly called the 'Sun Door' (or 'Golden Door' or 'Lion's Door'), is supposedly the door through which Jesus passed on Palm Sunday and where, according to religious tradition, the next Messiah should enter.

This tradition is linked to the Jubilee celebration (celebrated every 25 years since Pope Boniface VIII first celebrated it on 22 February 1300), which occurs in a Holy Year. On this occasion, the Pope or the Patriarch opens the Holy Doors. Lisbon Cathedral's Jubilee began to be celebrated in 1717, the year the Lisbon Patriarchate was founded.

Symbolically, the Holy Door represents Mary, or the 'Heavenly Gate' (*Portae Coelis*), as shown by the fleur-de-lys carved on the outside of the door and which signifies Divine Royalty. Passing through this Holy Door, that only the Cardinal Patriarch can open and use, symbolises the transition from mortality to immortality.

Finally, the Greek letters *alpha* and *omega*, also engraved on the door, symbolise the 'Beginning' and the 'End' and represent the Omnipotent God, Lord of Life and Death, through whom all things were created and will be reassembled, according to Saint John the Apostle in the New Testament (Revelations 1:4-8), and the Prophet Isaiah (44:6-8) in the Old Testament. In the Middle Ages, *alpha* and *omega* often decorated the Judge of the Universe's halo, to the right and left of his forehead. These two Greek letters are also commonly used to ornament Christian tombs to indicate that the person resting below saw his beginning and end in God.

The sacred symbolism of the Fleur-de-Lys

A symbol of Lisbon (Lis Boa or Boa Lis, as chronicler Fernão Lopes called it in 1434), the fleur-de-lys is symbolically linked to the iris and the lily (*Lilium*). According to Miranda Bruce-Mitford, Louis VII the Younger (1147) was the first king of France to adopt the iris as his emblem and use it as a seal for his letters patent (decrees). As the name Louis was then spelled Loys, it supposedly evolved to 'fleur-de-louis', then 'fleur-de-lys', its three petals representing Faith, Wisdom and Courage.

In reality, even if there is a strong resemblance between the iris and the fleur-de-lys, the French monarch merely adopted an ancient symbol of French heraldry.

In AD 496, an angel purportedly appeared before Clotilda (wife of Clovis, king of the Francs) and offered her a lily, an event that influenced her conversion to Christianity.

This miracle is also reminiscent of the story of the Virgin Mary, when the Angel Gabriel appeared to her, holding a lily, to tell her she was predestined to be the mother of the Saviour. This flower is also present in the iconography of Joseph, Christ's father, to designate him as the patriarch of the new holy dynasty of divine royalty.

In 1125, the French flag (and coat of arms) depicted a field of fleurs-de-lys. It remained unchanged until the reign of Charles V (1364), who officially adopted the symbol to honour the Holy Trinity, thus deciding to reduce the number of flowers to three. The flower's three petals also referred to the Trinity.

The lily stylised as a fleur-de-lys is also a biblical plant associated with the emblem of King David as well as Jesus Christ ('consider the lilies of the field ...' Matthew 6:28-29). It also appears in Egypt in association with the lotus flower, as well as in the Assyrian and Muslim cultures. It became an early symbol of power and sovereignty, and of the divine right of kings, also signifying the purity of body and soul. This is why the ancient kings of Europe were godly, consecrated by the Divinity through sacerdotal authority. Thus, theoretically, they were to be fair, perfect and pure beings as the Virgin Mary had been, she who is the 'Lily of the Annunciation and

Submission' (*Ecce Ancila Domine*, 'Here is the Servant of the Lord,' as Luke the Apostle reveals), and patron saint of all royal power.

The lily thus replaced the iris, which explains why, in Spanish, fleur-de-lys becomes *flor del lírio*, and why the two flowers are symbolically associated with the same lily. Botanically, the fleur-de-lys is neither an iris nor a lily. The iris (*Iris germanica*) is a plant of the Iridaceae family that originates in northern Europe. The more commonly known lily species (*Lilium pumilum*, *Lilium speciosum*, *Lilium candidum*) are members of the Liliaceae family that originates in Central Asia and Asia Minor.

The true fleur-de-lys belongs to neither the Iridaceae nor the Liliaceae family. It is the *Sprekelia formosissima*, a member of the Amaryllidaceae family that originates in Mexico and Guatemala. Known in other languages as the Aztec lily, the São Tiago lily, and the St James lily, *Sprekelia formosissima* is the only species of the genus. It was named in the 18th century by botanist Carl von Linné when he received a few bulbs from J. H. Van Sprekelsen, a German lawyer.

The Spanish introduced the plant to Europe when they brought bulbs back from Mexico at the end of the 16th century.

The monarchs and princes of Portugal knew of its symbolic meaning much earlier, however, since, roughly from the time of Afonso Henriques, and especially at the end of the 13th century, the lily, converted or stylised into the fleur-de-lys, appeared prominently on Portuguese coats of arms, with all its inherent, immediate and essential symbolism. This was entirely thanks to the Arab influence that brought it from Egypt to the Iberian Peninsula during the occupation.

𝔓our bi̋e

THE PENTAGRAMS OF
THE CATHEDRAL CLOISTER

The magic symbol of a medieval exorcism

Largo da Sé
Monday to Saturday, 10am–6pm
Tram 28E

The construction of Lisbon Cathedral's cloister, which is built in two architectural styles, Roman and Gothic, began during the reign of Dom Dinis (1279-1325). Above the arches can be found rosettes carved in the form of crosses, six-pointed and especially five-pointed stars.

The five-pointed star, or pentagram (which is represented in the same number of candleholders in front of the temple's main altar), is particularly significant here. In Christian iconography, it refers to Christ's five wounds on the Cross, but, due to its closed form, it is also identified with the circle represented by the coming together of the beginning and the end in Christ.

For the medieval Builder-Monks (p. 54), the pentagram signifies the realisation, the expression of the perfect, to the point that it became the sign of mutual recognition for the members of architectural guilds. They would draw the symbol on their letters as a form of salutation. The symbol's meaning was equivalent to that of the Latin word *vale* (be well) or *higia*, from the Greek goddess of health Hygia or Hygieia.

Here, the pentagram marks not only the productive presence of the medieval Builder-Monks, but is also the magic symbol of exorcism and protection against malicious influences, both visible and invisible. In the Middle Ages, it was a powerful talisman that represented Christ the Omnipotent, the Living God Himself, before which the malicious shadows revealed their impotence.

That is why the pentagram was used here as the protective symbol of the cloister, an expression of paradise or the 'Heavenly Jerusalem'.

Through its square form open to the celestial vault, the cloister represents the union between the Earth and the Heavens, symbolising Man's closeness to God.

Before the archaeological digs, a well and a tree stood in the garden at the centre of the cloister. The well represented the subterranean world, while the tree represented the celestial world.

The cloister thus illustrated the three levels of the cosmic centre of paradise or 'Heavenly Jerusalem' (subterranean, terrestrial, celestial) and was protected by the pentagram representing Christ.

THE BIRD PILLAR IN
THE CATHEDRAL CLOISTER

Birds, messengers of the holy word

Largo da Sé
Monday, 10am to 5pm ; Tuesday to Saturday, 10am to 7pm
Tram 28E

One of the sculpted capitals in Sé Cathedral cloister shows two birds drinking from a goblet. According to the Santa Cruz de Coimbra monastery's *Livro das Aves* (Book of Birds) and all medieval bestiaries, including Islamic bestiaries, birds are the messengers of the holy word (see also Ecclesiastes 10:20). In Roman art, birds feed on holy bread (gnosis) and royal blood (illumination) – a reference to the Eucharist – in the holy vessel (*Saint Vaisel*).

Thanks to the art of troubadours and minstrels, medieval spirituality celebrated this vessel under the name of the Holy Grail. On this capital, one bird raises its beak while swallowing holy bread, thus illustrating how the soul rises towards the mysteries of God's wisdom. The other bird drinks royal blood from the goblet, thus showing the same soul embodied by the grace of the Holy Spirit.

THE OFF-AXIS COLUMN OF SÉ CATHEDRAL

⑬

A reminder of the 1755 earthquake

Largo da Sé
Monday to Saturday, 10am–6pm
Tram 28E

The oldest part of the Sé cathedral is the ambulatory, with its radiating chapels. On the right, between the chapels of Saint Sebastian and Our Lady of Pity, look carefully at the base on which the outermost column (on the ambulatory side) rests: you will notice that the column is not perfectly centred on its support.

This unusual detail is the result of the 1755 earthquake, which caused the column to shift on its axis.

PILLAR OF THE SOULS

A symbol of the ascension of human souls

Largo da Sé
Monday, 10am–5pm; Tuesday to Saturday, 10am–7pm
Tram 28E

I n Sé Cathedral cloister, built in the 13th century under the reign of Dom Dinis, a strange Gothic pillar shows carved figures rising in a spiral manner from the base to the top. Taken from one of the cloister's deconsecrated chapels, the pillar is a symbol of the ascension of human souls from the Earth to the Heavens. These souls, depending on the amount of virtue they possess, are in constant danger of falling into hell, or, at best, of spending an indeterminate period of time in purgatory. *The Pillar of the Souls* also shows the four social classes of the Middle Ages (clergy, nobility, bourgeoisie, and the peasants) as they begin the St James' Way pilgrimage from Lisbon to the Cathedral of Santiago de Compostela in Spain, which was the most important pilgrimage at the time. All social classes participated – priests and bishops, kings and nobles, but most of all the lower classes. They all tried to pay for their sins and obtain indulgences.

ROMAN STELAE
AT PEDRAS NEGRAS

History on every street corner

Travessa das Pedras Negras, Largo da Madalena, 1–3
Tram 12E, 28E – Metro Rossio, Baixa-Chiado or Terreiro do Paço

Known as the Almada building, this example of Pombaline-style architecture at No. 1-3 travessa das Pedras Negras was built in 1749 by Dom João de Almada de Melo, Senhor de Souto d'El-Rei. On the side wall, at the angle that the building forms with rua das Pedras Negras, a row of four white stones decorates the facade.

Close up, these stones reveal Latin inscriptions that indicate their origins. They are Roman stelae, probably dedicated to the deities Mercury and Cybele. A temple to Cybele is thought to have been built here in the 2nd century AD.

These four stelae, unearthed during restoration work on the foundations of the building (classified as a national monument in 1910), are part of the great archaeological discoveries from the Roman era in Lisbon. Others are the *Galerias Romanas* on rua da Prata (cryptoportico or covered gallery, opened to the public only once a year by the City Council); *Núcleo Arqueológico da Rua dos Correiros* (the archaeological site discovered in 1995 during the renovation of a building); and the remains of an ancient Roman theatre in the nearby patio d'Aljube. Built at the time of the Emperor Augustus in the 1st century, rebuilt on Nero's orders, dismantled during the reign of Constantine and finally abandoned in the 4th century, the theatre was rediscovered in 1798.

Among the wording half-erased by time, some letters can still be made out. On the first stele is the incomplete inscription MERCVUR ... / CAESA ... / AVGVST ... / C. IVLIVS F. IU ... / PERMISS V. DEC ... /

DEDIT. F, from which only the name Caius Julius and invocations to the god Mercury and the emperor Caesar Augustus can be deciphered. In addition to its inscription, the second stele has a section of column and a small pedestal. The following characters are legible: DEVM MATR / T. LICINIVS / AMARANTIVS / V.S.L.M., which can be interpreted as 'Titus Licinius Amaranthus, in honour of the mother of the gods'.

A larger stele, over two-metres-high, bears the inscription L. CAECILIO. L.F. CELERI. RECTO. / QVAEST. PROVINC. BAET.7 TRIB. PLEB. PRAETORI. FEL. IVL. / OLISIPO, which means 'Felicitas Julia Olisipo pays tribute to Lucius Caecilius, son of Lucius Celeri, rector, quaestor of the province of Betica, tribune of the people and praetor'. This tribute from the people of Lisbon to the praetor Lucius Caecilius, from the province of present-day Andalucia, testifies to Lisbon's importance for Julius Caesar.

The last stele takes the form of a small pediment where the following is written: MATRI DE / VM MAG, IDAE / A FRHYG. T. L./LYCH CERNO / P.H.R. PERN. IIVI / CASS. ET CASS. STA./M. AT. ET AP. COSS. GAI. This is a dedication by Caius Licinius Cerno – originally from Lycaonia, an ancient region of Asia Minor – in reference to the Phrygian Mount Ida, Cybele's shrine.

The magical 'black stones'

The Pedras Negras (Black Stones) place name comes from the Early Roman road, made from black stones, which led to the temple of the goddess Cybele.

These stones had a magical purpose: the ancients believed that they channelled the Earth's telluric energy, and that the space around the temple was powerfully magnetised thanks to the concentrated forces that the stones prevented from dispersing. The colour black also indicated the initial stage of a spiritual journey ending at the gates of the shrine.

Olisipo: Lisbon's version of the Goddess Cybele

Cybele was a Phrygian goddess whose cult began in Asia Minor and spread to Ancient Greece under the name Potnia Theron (Mistress of the Animals). The Romans called her Mater Deum Magna (Great Mother of the Gods) and here in Olisipo, the Roman Lisbon, she was 'nationalised' and identified with the Graeco-Iberian goddess Ulisipa, mythical founder of the city. Cybele was depicted with a mural crown, an allegory of her protective military power, alongside lions symbolising imperial power; or sometimes in a chariot drawn by these wild beasts, and holding a cornucopia, symbol of fertility and opulence. It is believed that the cult of Cybele in Lisbon was aimed at three distinct social groups: soldiers responsible for the defence of the city and who recognised her as the *genius loci* (protective spirit); politicians who demanded wealth and honours from her; and women who prayed for fertility and a healthy pregnancy.

Baixa, Rossio

THE MYSTERIOUS *CAIS DAS COLUNAS*

The Masonic entrance for the future 'emperor of the world'?

Metro Terreiro do Paço

The *Cais das Colunas* (quay of the Columns) got its name from two monolithic pillars that stand at each end of the *Praça do Comércio* (Market square), designed by architect Eugénio dos Santos during the city's reconstruction after the earthquake of 1755.

These biblically inspired and clearly Masonic columns are identical to the *Jakim* (Wisdom) and *Bohaz* (Devotion) columns of Solomon's Temple. The *Cais das Colunas* opens onto the Tagus and its Atlantic estuary, beyond which lie other continents, civilisations and cultures. It is thus the world's gateway to Lisbon, which is why, quite early on, the Sebastianists believed that the 'Secret King' (also called the emperor of the world or the 'Desired One' – see p. 100) would eventually disembark here, arriving from the 'Island of Utopia'. The Royal House of the Freemasons of Lusitania probably used the myth to have Masonic columns placed on the quay. Right across from the quay, an equestrian statue of Dom José I stands in the middle of the square facing the quay, ready to announce the arrival of the universal emperor. Behind him, the Augusta street arch opens Lisbon to the world. The underlying concept of the architectural and artistic design of the entire Praça do Comércio is to personalise the divine attributes of the last *sephiroth* (sphere) of the Judaeo-Christian Kabbalah's Tree of Life (see p. 185), *Malkuth*, the symbol of 'Reign' and the 'World.' The *Cais das Colunas* thus becomes the entrance to the 'Temple of the Desired One' that the square represents; the Augusta street arch is the gate to the 'City of Mysteries'.

No written document has been found that mentions the year the *Cais das Colunas* was built. All that is known is that it was completed at the end of the 18th century because it features in a colour engraving by Noel and Wells entitled *A view of the Praça do Comércio at Lisbon*, dating

from 1792. The columns collapsed at the end of the 19th century and were not replaced until 1929. Dismantled in early 1997 for works related to the extension of the metro between Chiado and Santa Apolónia, the *Cais das Colunas* regained its rightful place on the Terreiro do Paço or Praça do Comércio on 25 August 2008.

Baixa Pombalina's sacred architecture

Covering an area of 23.5 hectares, the Baixa Pombalina district came into being after the earthquake of 1755 through the efforts of the Marquis of Pombal (see p. 249), the Minister of Public Works of King Dom José I. His drafts show a square-shaped network that was built by two corporations: the *Casa dos 24* (House of 24), founded in 1383, and the *Casa Real dos Maçons da Lusitânia* (Royal House of the Builders of Lusitania), founded in 1733. In 1716, under Dom João V, Lisbon had already been divided into two parts: east and west. Following hermetic tradition (see below), the Marquis of Pombal also kept the city's 12 pre-existing neighbourhoods (which were thus numerically equal to the 12 signs of the zodiac) reflected by the 7 hills representing the 7 traditional planets. He also planned 17 large avenues, thus using the number 17, which is a key number for Portugal (see p. 98). Three main avenues lead from *Terreiro do Paço* (Palace terrace), rua Augusta (in the centre), *rua do Ouro* and *rua da Prata* (on either side). They symbolise the caduceus representing Mercury, which is composed of a central column around which two snakes, one black and one white, intertwine; one snake is solar (golden) and the other lunar (silver). These serpents

(*ofiússas*) represent the arteries through which vital energy flows. The lunar artery is cold and passive, while the solar one is hot and active. In traditional symbolism, gold represents the Sun and silver the Moon. *Rua do Ouro* (Gold street) thus corresponds to the caduceus' solar aspect, while *rua da Prata* (Silver street) corresponds to its lunar aspect. As for *rua Augusta*, it symbolises the central column, the channel that fuses and synthesises the two polar forces.

Hermetism: Reflecting the organisation of the cosmos on earth to attract celestial energy

As described in the works of Hermes Trismegistus (which were long considered to be Egyptian), the hermetic tradition believes that reproducing the organisation of the heavens (stars, planets, etc.) on Earth (in the design of a city or the ceiling of a room, for example) is a way of attracting divine energy to the place in question.

The seven sacred hills of Lisbon

According to one of the popular legends about the origins of Lisbon, the city was founded by Ulysses who fell in love with Ofiússa, the queen of the snake-women. When Homer's hero returned to his Greek homeland aboard the *Argos*, thus abandoning Ofiússa, she was so furious that she made the plateau of Ulisibona (or Olisipo), now Lisbon, tremble. From her rattles sprang the seven hills of the city. The tradition, a blend of myth and prophecy popular with Lisbon residents, declares that the seven hills of Lisbon refer to the seven gates of Heavenly Jerusalem, as represented by Lisbon's seven principal Christian temples which stand at the top of each hill: São Cristóvão, São Vicente de Fora e Sé Velha, São José da Anunciada, Nossa Senhora da Graça, Chagas de Cristo, Santa Catarina, and São Roque. The idea of transferring the sacred meaning of the seven hills of Jerusalem (Gared, Goath, Acra, Bezetha, Moriah, Ophel and Zion) and of Rome (Campidoglio, Quirinale, Viminale, Esquilino, Celio, Aventino and Palatino) to Lisbon, coinciding with the Sun's course from east to west, is a very ancient one. However, it took on an elaborate form in the works of 17th-century Portuguese authors such as Frei Nicolau de Oliveira, who superimposed Lisbon's greatness on that of Rome. The capital's seven hills (an allegory of the seven elements of matter: atomic particles, subatomic particles, ether, air, fire, water, earth) are: São Jorge in Mouraria; São Vicente in Alfama; Santa Ana in Anunciada; Santo André in Graça; Chagas in Carmo; Santa Catarina next to Largo de Camões; and São Roque in Bairro Alto. The Tagus river flows at the foot of the seven hills. According to the sacred tradition, it thus symbolises the river of Paradise (*Paradhesa*) that bathes the seven spiritual poles (*Qutbs* or *Chakras* in Arab and Sanskrit) that bring life to the seven primordial lands (*Aqtabs* or *Dwipas*, in Arab and Sanskrit).

Hermes Trismegistus and hermetism

Hermes Trismegistus, which in Latin means 'thrice-great Hermes', is the name given by the neo-Platonists, alchemists, and hermetists to the Egyptian god *Thot*, Hermes to the Greeks. In the Old Testament, he is also identified with the patriarch Enoch. In their respective cultures, all three were considered to be the creators of phonetic writing, theurgical magic, and messianic prophetism.

Thot was connected to the lunar cycles whose phases expressed the harmony of the universe.

Egyptian writings refer to him as 'twice great' because he was the god of the Word and of Wisdom. In the syncretic atmosphere of the Roman Empire, the epithet of the Egyptian god *Thot* was given to the Greek god Hermes, but this time was 'thrice great' (*trismegistus*) for the Word, Wisdom and his duty as Messenger of all the gods of Elysium or Olympus. The Romans associated him with *Mercury*, the planet that mediates between the Earth and the Sun, which is a function that Kabbalistic Jews called *Metraton* (see p. 183), the 'perpendicular measure between the Earth and the Sun'.

In Hellenic Egypt, Hermes was the 'scribe and messenger of the gods' and was believed to be the author of a collection of sacred texts, called *hermetic*, that contained teachings about art, science, religion and philosophy – the *Corpus Hermeticum* – the objective of which was the deification of humanity through knowledge of God. These texts, which were probably written by a group belonging to the *Hermetic School* of ancient Egypt, thus express the knowledge accumulated over time by attributing it to the god of Wisdom, who is in all points similar to the Hindu god *Ganesh*.

The *Corpus Hermeticum*, which probably dates from the 1st to the 3rd centuries AD, represented the source of inspiration of hermetic and neo-Platonic thought during the Renaissance. Even though Swiss scholar Casaubon had apparently proved the contrary in the 17th century, people continued to believe that the text dated back to Egyptian antiquity before Moses and that it announced the coming of Christianity.

According to Clement of Alexandria, it contained 42 books divided into six volumes. The first treated the education of priests; the second, the rites of the temple; the third, geology, geography, botany and agriculture; the fourth, astronomy and astrology, mathematics and architecture; the fifth contained hymns to the glory of the gods and a guide of political action for kings; the sixth was a medical text.

It is generally believed that Hermes Trismegistus invented a card game full of esoteric symbols, of which the first 22 were made of blades of gold and the 56 others of blades of silver – the *tarot* or 'Book of Thot'. Hermes is also attributed with writing the *Book of the Dead* or 'Book of the Exit towards the Light,' as well as the famous alchemy text *The Emerald Table*, works that had a strong influence on the alchemy and magic practised in medieval Europe. In medieval Europe, especially between the 5th and 14th centuries, hermetism was also a School of Hermeneutics that interpreted certain poems of antiquity and various enigmatic myths and works of art as allegorical treaties of alchemy or hermetic science. For this reason, the term hermetism still designates the esoteric nature of a text, work, word or action, in that they possess an occult meaning that requires a hermeneutic, or in other words a philosophical science, to correctly interpret the hidden meaning of the object of study.

Hermetic principles were adopted and applied by the Roman *Colegium Fabrorum*, associations of the architects of civil, military and religious constructions. This knowledge was transmitted in the 12th century to the Christian *Builder-Monks*, the builders of the grand Roman and Gothic edifices of Europe, who executed their work according to the principles of sacred architecture, true to the model of sacred geometry. It is the direct legacy of volumes three and four of the *Corpus Hermeticum*, according to which cities and buildings were constructed in interrelation with specific planets and constellations, so that the design of the Heavens could be reproduced on Earth, thus favouring cosmic or sidereal energies. All of this was done with the purpose of achieving the hermetic principle that states: 'Everything above is like everything below'.

During the European Renaissance (16th and 17th centuries), hermetism was replaced by humanism. Forms were rationalised and the transcendental ignored. It was the end of the traditional society and the beginning of a profane, Baroque and pre-modernist society, paving the way for the arrival of the materialism and atheism that dominates the modern world.

There were, however, some exceptions to this predominant rule in Europe. In Portugal, in the 16th century, the *Master Builders*, the heirs of the Builder-Monks, founded the Manueline style (see p. 180) according to the hermetic rules of sacred architecture. The influence of the *Free Builders* continued into the 18th century and their greatest work was the restoration of Lisbon after the earthquake of 1755. That is why Pombal's Lisbon is designed and constructed according to the geometric and architectural measures of the Tradition handed down by Hermes Trismegistus.

SYMBOLS OF THE EQUESTRIAN STATUE OF KING DOM JOSÉ I

Praça do Comércio and Mafra convent, at the heart of theories about the Fifth Empire?

Praça do Comércio
Metro Terreiro do Paço

At the centre of Terreiro do Paço stands the equestrian statue of King Dom José I (1714-1777) designed by Machado de Castro and cast by Bartolomeu da Costa, and which was inaugurated on the king's birthday (6 June 1775). The statue's location was imposed by Eugénio dos Santos' design. It occupies the geometric centre of an equilateral triangle whose corners point to the Augusta street arch and the lateral gates of the two large towers that complement the square's openness. It is interesting to note that, when you superimpose the layout of Mafra convent on that of Terreiro do Paço, the apse and the statue of the Lusitanian emperor stand at exactly the same spot, and the convent's two large towers are at the same latitude as those of the square.

Some people have concluded that the proportions of the two locations are equal and complementary, their intention being to situate the temporal capital of the world here, and the spiritual capital seven leagues away at Mafra, in accordance with the conception of the inspired ideology of the Fifth Lusitanian Empire (see p. 64). This *translatio imperii* theme is also present in the remarkable bas-relief on the back of the statue's base. Here, the crowned Child, near his mother, receives Lisbon's coat of arms from defeated Rome. At his feet lies a treasure-filled chest that a dignitary is offering him, while an architect shows the design of New Lisbon to the Virgin Mary.

At the top of the monument, Dom José I, dressed in 'Roman style' with a cape of the Order of Christ and holding the imperial sceptre, sits astride a horse that is crushing serpents (*ofiússas*), an iconic symbol of *São Jorge*, to whom the monarch was devoted. Here, he takes on the role of God's king-priest (see p. 64) who, it is said, will govern the Fifth Empire of the World from Lisbon, which explains why his face is turned towards the Tagus estuary and why he looks towards distant continents.

Below, on the sides, *Triumph* (horse) and *Renown* (elephant) symbolise the West and the East. The *Renown* of the East (the ancient era) transfers its true values to the *Triumph* of the West (the new era). The trumpeter angel near the elephant and the angel holding a palm leaf near the horse dominate the old man, who represents the profane. They symbolise the spiritual traditions of the East and West uniting in Lisbon.

FERNANDO PESSOA'S TABLE

Where Pessoa dreamed of the 'Fifth Empire'

Martinho da Arcada café-restaurant
Metro Terreiro do Paço

The Martinho da Arcada café-restaurant will always be linked with one of its regular customers, Fernando Pessoa, who wrote most of his poems there, including those of the only book he published during his lifetime – *Mensagem*.

In a quiet corner, enjoying a cup of coffee, a glass of brandy and a cigarette, he evoked Bandarra and António Vieira, dreamt of a secret king and a Fifth Empire, and tried to reveal and announce Portugal's greatest destiny with certitude (see p. 64).

To honour the greatest contemporary defender of the Portuguese language, the manager of Martinho da Arcada has left the table and chair where the poet habitually sat. Photographs and autographs of the author surround it. Today, it is the inevitable meeting place for the literary gatherings of Pessoa specialists and admirers. Some of them, and more than just a few, are so immersed in their passion that they have adopted the poet's mannerisms.

Fernando Pessoa

There is no clear evidence proving that poet and essayist Fernando António Nogueira Pessoa (Lisbon, 13 June 1888 – Lisbon, 30 November 1935) was, in fact, a Freemason, even if nowadays many factions of this institution claim to be the poet-prophet's followers. Fernando Pessoa had an early interest in occultism and even frequented this milieu between 1910 and 1920, driven by the desire to know more about the mysteries of life. This was how he came into contact with spiritualism and theosophy in 1912 and began translating English theosophical books into Portuguese in 1915. An astrology buff, he set himself up as an astrologer in Lisbon in January 1916, under the pseudonym Rafael Baldaya, completing more than a thousand horoscopes. Pessoa's insatiable thirst for knowledge, together with his great familiarity with occultism, led him to develop his thinking based on the notion of spiritual 'Portugueseness', linked to the coming of the Fifth Empire (see p. 64). At the time of António Salazar's rise to power and the establishment of the *Estado Novo* in 1933, Fernando Pessoa quickly declared himself against Salazar, especially when his essays and poems began to be censored. He then wrote a series of anti-Salazar poems. Salazar decided to abolish all the Initiatory Orders and spiritual movements in Portugal. When deputy José Cabral's bill prohibiting secret associations and, notably, Portuguese Freemasonry, was presented before Parliament, Fernando Pessoa publicly opposed it in a brilliant article published in the *Diário de Lisboa* on 4 February 1935. In defence of the religious freedom and traditional spirit that characterised Freemasonry, he declared, 'I am not a Freemason and I belong to no other order, similar or not. Yet I am not anti-Freemasonry either, for what I do know about it persuades me to be fully in favour of it.' Because of this article, Fernando Pessoa remains connected to Freemasonry. There are even lodges that bear his name, despite the fact that he was never a member. He was simply a fervent defender of the freedom of expression and of religious worship, whether it be Freemasonry or some other leaning. Finally, in his work 'Identity Card', written in Lisbon on 30 March 1935, Fernando Pessoa openly revealed his position on spirituality. *'Religious opinion: Christian gnostic and consequently opposed to all organised churches, and especially the Church of Rome. Loyal to the secret tradition of Christianity that is intimately linked to the secret tradition of Israel (the Holy Kabbalah) and to the occult spirit of Freemasonry. Initiatory position: initiated, directly from Master to Disciple, in the three inferior degrees of the Knights Templar of Portugal (apparently abolished).'* At last, as Fernando Pessoa summed up in his poem 'São João' (9 June 1935), 'If you are a Freemason, I am more – I am a Templar'.

THE SYMBOLS OF LISBON'S TRIUMPHAL ARCH

The Rosicrucians in Lisbon

Metro Terreiro do Paço

Although many European cities possess a triumphal arch representing the Temporal Empire, Lisbon's arch represents, above all, the idea of the Spiritual Empire. Indeed, it appears to have been built so that, one day, the Secret Universal Emperor may pass through it, thus inaugurating a New Age for the world in Lisbon, according to the Fifth Empire tradition. From this mythic and sacred point of view, this triumphal arch thus represents the symbolic, final door towards humanity's last *translatio imperii* (see p. 64). Symbolically, the arch

evokes the threshold of mysteries, and the doorway from the shadows of ignorance to the Light of Wisdom that mythical Lisbon conceals. It announces the spiritual Resurrection, as signalled by the Saint Andrew's cross with, at its centre, the secret king's rose, which can be seen at the interior crown of the arch. The arch's rear facade, on the Augusta street side, displays an enormous clock that fatally marks the time until the coming of the Fifth Empire. The rose and Saint Andrew's cross indicate that the Free Builders of the Marquis of Pombal period, who rebuilt New Lisbon after the earthquake of 1755, were inspired by the mysticism of the ancient Rosicrucians, followers of primitive Christianity. The Rosicrucians appeared in Portugal in 1700, first hidden by the Franciscan piety of the Espírito Santo de Mafra convent where they resided, then revealed in 1717, by the Casa Real dos Maçons Lusitanos (Royal House of the Lusitanian Freemasons). No sooner had Lisbon been rebuilt than these mystic followers disappeared from Portuguese history books. Some say they went to establish the city of Washington, D.C. in the United States, whose layout is largely inspired by that of Lisbon (see the *Secret Washington D.C.* guide by the same publisher). The triumphal arch of Augusta street is a monumental accomplishment, on the scale of Pombal-period architecture. It was not entered in an architectural competition until 1843, under the Costa Cabral government, and not built until 1862. It was finally completed in 1873, thanks to a project by Veríssimo José da Costa and the intervention of Vítor Bastos and the Frenchman A.C. Camels.

Camels' sculpture, which tops the monument, represents Glorious Lusitania, shown as the Great Universal Mother, rewarding Apollo and Minerva (Inspiration and Understanding) or, in another interpretation, 'Glory crowing Genius and Valour'.

The transfer of power – Translatio Imperii

The Latin expression *translatio imperii*, which means both 'succession of empires' and 'transfer of power', is a concept created in Europe in the Middle Ages to describe history as a linear phenomenon – a succession of transfers of power from a supreme governing power, or *imperador*, to the next, who controls the imperio, and which is marked by well-defined cycles. Generally, authors described the *translatio imperii* as a succession that resulted in placing the supreme power in the hands of the king or emperor who ruled the region in which they lived. They established the spiritual and temporal origin of their country leading to the establishment of imperial power by incorporating former cultures that had contributed to the development of the country's religious, cultural and social characteristics. Some notable examples are:

Otto de Freising (who lived in what is now Germany, from 1114 to 1158): Rome → Byzantium → the Francs → the Lombards → the Germans (the Holy Roman Germanic Empire);

Chrétien de Troyes (who lived in medieval France, from 1135 to 1190): Greece → Rome → France (the Frankish Empire);

Richard de Bury (England, 1287-1345): Athens → Rome → Paris → London (the Franco-Breton Empire).

The authors of the Middle Ages and the Renaissance legitimated this transfer of power through a relationship between a royal figure and a

god or hero of Greek or Roman antiquity, as Virgil had done when he made Aeneas (a Trojan hero) the mythical founder of the city of Rome in the *Aeneid*. Following the same tradition, in the 12th century, the Anglo-Norman authors Geoffrey of Monmouth (in his *Historia Regnum Britanniae*) and Wace (in *Brut*) attributed the founding of Great Britain to the arrival of Brutus of Troy, the son of Aeneas. In the same manner, the French Renaissance writer, Jean Lemaire de Belges (in his *Illustrations of Gaul and the Singularities of Troy*), connected the founding of Celtic Gaul to the arrival of the Trojan, Francus, son of Hector, and that of Celtic Germany to the arrival of Bavo, Priam's cousin. Thus, an illustrious genealogy was established for Pepin and Charlemagne (the legend of Francus was the basis for Ronsard's epic poem *La Franciade*). The erudite origin of the Lusitanian *translatio imperii* lies in the works of the Cistercian Joachim of Fiore (see

p. 190), born in Calabria (Italy) around 1132. In his work *Liber Figurarum*, he divides the world into three universal ages: that of the Father, the Son and the Holy Spirit. The first is situated in the past in Jerusalem, the second in the present in Rome, and the third in the future in Lisbon. Joachim of Fiore drew his inspiration from the Old Testament texts of the prophet Daniel in which Daniel interprets the dream of a statue of King Nebuchadnezzar as an early vision of Paradise on Earth. Several writers have justified Portugal's particular mission by referring to the following verse from the scriptures: 'For so hath the Lord commanded us, saying, I have set thee to be a light of the Gentiles, that thou shouldest be for salvation unto the ends of the earth' (Acts 13:47). An astute expert on the subject, Luís de Camões (1525-1580) also prophesied about Lisbon a little later, in *Os Lusíadas* (The Lusiads), VI, 7 (from the 1776 translation by William Julius Mickle, published in 1877): 'Resolv'd in Lisbon glorious to renew / The Roman honours – raging with despair / From high Olympus' brow he cleaves the air / On earth new hopes of vengeance to devise / And sue that aid denied him in the skies.'

Using the same principle, the idea of transferring the sacred meaning of the seven hills of Jerusalem and Rome to Lisbon (see p. 53), following the path of the sun from east to west, also took on an elaborate form among the Portuguese authors of the 17th century, such as Frei Nicolau de Oliveira. Finally, Joachim of Fiore's three ages of the world concept was reformulated by Father António Vieira (1608-1697) (see p. 66) who wrote of five ages, the last being the Fifth Portuguese Empire, the future spiritual and temporal Fifth Empire of Humanity of which Lisbon would be the birthplace. The preceding empires were the Assyrian, Persian, Greek and Roman; the Portuguese empire will be the last. The first empire (Assyrian) was ruled by the Father; the second (Persian) by the Father and the Son; the third (Greek) by the Son; the fourth (Roman) by the Son and the Holy Spirit; the fifth (Lusitanian) will be ruled by the Holy Spirit, symbolised by the 'return of Dom Sebastian' (see p. 100), a simple allegorical representation of the true king and priest of God, Christ, who will have Lusitania ('Land of Light') for the *Parousie* (presence/return of the Lord).

Absolutely identical to the Egyptian obelisk of Rome's Piazza Navona fountain, the Necessidades obelisk-fountain, on Largo do Rilvas, is a clear reference to the principle of the *translatio imperii* from Rome to Lisbon, which, according to myth, was to occur sometime after 2005 during the astrological era of Aquarius and would inaugurate a new period of progress for humanity.

Father António Vieira and the fifth empire

Father António Vieira was born to a family of humble origins on rua do Cónego, near Sé Cathedral (a commemorative plaque has been placed next to the front door of the house) in Lisbon on 6 February 1608. He was the eldest of the four children of Cristovão Vieira Ravasco, originally from Alentejo (his mother was the daughter of an African/European mulatto woman), and Maria de Azevedo, a Lisbon native. Cristovão served in the Portuguese navy and was a clerk for the Inquisition for two years. He left for Brazil, alone, in 1609, to fill the clerk's position at Salvador da Bahia; his family later joined him. António Vieira arrived in Bahia at the age of six and began his schooling at Salvador's Jesuit school. A rather disastrous student at first, 'thanks to the intervention of Our Lady', he became the most brilliant. Legend says that one day when he skipped school, an angel appeared to him to show him the way back. In May 1623, when he had just entered the Society of Jesus as a novice and was having great difficulty acquiring the required knowledge, he prayed, crying, to the Virgin Mary, asking her to inspire him. He felt a shock and fainted. When he regained consciousness, he found himself gifted with a remarkable intelligence that made him a striking figure of his time.

Indeed, António Vieira was the most influential person of the 17th century in Portugal and Brazil. A monk of rare spirituality, an inspired writer and passionate orator, he was also a great humanist defender of the rights of the oppressed. In politics, he distinguished himself as a missionary in Brazil where he tirelessly defended the rights of the indigenous people, fighting against their exploitation and enslavement. In return, they gave him the name Paiaçu (meaning 'Grand Father' in the Tupi language).

Following his humanist code of ethics in Portugal, António Vieira also defended the Jews, the abolition of the distinction between New Christians (converted Jews, persecuted by the Inquisition) and old Christians (traditional Catholics), and the abolition of slavery. In fact, he strongly criticised the priests of his period and the Inquisition.

He was an early follower of the ideal of Sebastianism and again entered into conflict with the Inquisition, which accused him of heresy based on a 1659 letter in which he explained his theory of the Fifth Empire and Portugal's future supremacy in this great future empire to the Bishop of Japan. He was thrown out of Lisbon, banished and imprisoned in Porto, then in Coimbra. In 1667, he was condemned to imprisonment and was prohibited from preaching, but six months later the sentence was annulled.

He returned to Brazil in 1681 and there compiled his writings in order to publish the 16 volumes of his Sermons and to complete the Clavis Prophetarum, the key of the prophecies exposed throughout his works, and notably in his *História do futuro* (*History of the Future*), a work in which he presents the five Ages of the World, Lusitania being the dominating element of the final age. He published more than 500 letters in three volumes. In literature, his Sermons are considered to be of capital importance for the Portuguese and Brazilian Baroque period.

In 1694, elderly and feeble, he was no longer able to write. On 10 June, his last suffering began and he lost his voice. He died on 18 July 1697, aged 89, at the Jesuit School in Salvador da Bahia.

Portugal: the 'head' of the 'body' of Europe?

The fact that Europe is sometimes seen as a *Body* comes from a 14th-century map (1335-37) by Opicinius de Canestris; three different versions of the map are known today. Later, Sebastian Münster, the Franciscan of Basel, published a map in his work *Cosmography* that was largely inspired by this medieval map. His colleague and fellow countryman, Heinrich Bünting, published it, with a few additions, in his main work *Itinerarium Sacrae Scripturae*, and again in his work *Pro Hispaniae Defensio* with the corrections of Portuguese humanist Damião de Góis. In the 17th century (1624), Julião de Castro, in his *History of the Goths*, makes Europe a woman of whom Spain is the head and Portugal, her crown. This provoked, in 1631, the following comment by António de Souza Macedo in his *Flores de España, Excelencias de Portugal*: 'which is honoured in Portugal, because if there are heads that honour certain crowns, in general it is the crown that honours the head.'

In this notion, taken up by Fernando Pessoa in his poem *O dos castelos* (The Castles) from the book *Mensagem* (Message), and by Camões in Song III, verses 17 and 20 of *Os Lusíadas*, the Iberian Peninsula is thus the head of Europe and the Italian peninsula (which is boot-shaped) is its feet. The head, or the coordinator, and the feet almost touch while the arms are thrown back, as if ready to jump into the waters of the Atlantic; the Portuguese 'face' fixedly stares at the American horizon. Each country corresponds to one of the other organs.

Although all the ancient versions of maps unanimously place Portugal at the head of Europe, they sometimes differ in the placement of some countries, even if the commonly held positions are the following: the feet and the legs are in the Italian peninsula while the genital region is in the Balkans. The base of the spine is also

positioned there and is thus connected to Eastern Europe, the zone from which creative energy (called *Kundalinî* in the East) emanates. Austria-Hungary is the solar plexus, the navel region, and the intestines, and is also connected to the East. The lungs are linked to Switzerland and Central Europe, the zone of fiduciary circulation (money, capital) that makes the entire trade sector function. The heart is in France and Luxembourg (the word *Luxembourg*, like *Lusitania*, means 'place of light' – it is from Luxembourg that the founders of the Portucalense earldom came, this place where all the doctrines blend harmoniously). The arms are in the industrial zone of Northern Europe (Germany, the Low Countries, Britain and Scandinavia), which represents the working Europe. The head is the zone that stretches from the Pyrenees to the extreme west of the Iberian Peninsula, Portugal (and Galicia) representing the crowned face and the forehead of all Europe. It may therefore be concluded that Portugal mentally and spiritually drives Europe, which, for the greatest harmony for everything and everyone, should encourage Culture, the spirit of Portugal.

Note also that, in the body, the brain dominates the inferior organs, even if they obviously also have the power to affect it, and that, when the brain dies, the entire body dies along with it.

THE BLAZING EAGLE
OF SÃO NICOLAU

*A symbol of the city's rebirth after the
1755 earthquake*

Corner of Augusta and São Nicolau streets

At the corner of Augusta and São Nicolau streets, people often walk by without noticing the uncommon silhouette of an eagle among flames. The high relief is most likely the work of sculptor Joaquim Machado de Castro or his assistant, Francisco Leal Garcia, as they were the sculptors of the reconstruction of the Baixa Pombalina district after the 1755 earthquake. Like the mythical phoenix rising from its ashes, the eagle of Lisbon (in antiquity, Portugal was represented by an eagle, which was also the imperial emblem of Lisbon) rose from the destructive fires caused by the terrible earthquake of 1755.

The eagle: the only bird with double eyelids capable of staring directly at the Sun

For the Greeks and Persians, the eagle, which is capable of staring directly at the Sun, was linked to the Sun and Jupiter. The Egyptians called the eagle Ah and dedicated it to the god Horus, and by extension Osiris, while the Copts venerated it under the name of Aham. For the Greeks, the eagle was the sacred emblem of Zeus, and for the Druids, it represented the Supreme God. Medieval bestiaries compared the eagle with Adam, the Father of Humanity, because, in the beginning, he lived near God. This symbol has survived to modern times thanks to the crowned heads of Europe. Following the example of the Roman general Marius (who made the two-headed eagle the emblem of Imperial Rome in the 2nd century BC), they chose this king of the air to represent their families. The two-headed eagle was also the emblem of the royal families of Russia, Poland, Austria and Germany. Jupiter, however, was satisfied with a one-headed eagle, as was the blazing Sun. Such is also the case for the eagle on Augusta street, which symbolises the indivisible unity of the Spirit of Christ whose ascension is sometimes illustrated by an eagle. The eagle flies at high altitudes and looks directly at the Sun, just like the Son before God the Eternal Father.

ROSSIO CINEMA'S ART NOUVEAU FACADE

A vestige of the first 'luminous projections using Drumont's light'

Rua dos Sapateiros, 229

The Animatógrafo do Rossio (Rossio cinematograph) is the last survivor of the grand epic of the birth of cinema in Portugal.

Located on rua dos Sapateiros (Cobbler street), near the Arco do Bandeira (Flag Arch) that opens on to Praça do Rossio, this cinematograph opened on 8 December 1907.

With more than 100 seats, this theatre in the city centre was first known as the Rossio Palace. In addition to serving as a cinema, it was also a children's theatre. The stage, like all the interior decor, is in Art Nouveau style, with balustrades and small forged iron gates separating the stage from the orchestra pit.

It is said that the children's theatre company, 'Tim-Tim por Tim-Tim', sponsored by Baron Henrique Álvaro Antunes da Silva Neves, eventually disbanded in Lisbon after a final performance here at Rossio Palace.

The company had even travelled to perform in São Salvador da Bahia, Brazil, where it had achieved great success at the Teatro São João at the turn of the 20th century.

Now a pornographic cinema, the building has preserved a few traces of its past splendour and greatness on its main facade. The Art Nouveau decor and two polychrome azulejo panels, signed 'M. Queriol, 1907' and made in collaboration with Jorge Pinto in his Ajuda workshop, are especially noteworthy.

The first 'luminous projections using Drumont's light' – the first film projections – took place in Lisbon on 10 December 1894, on the second floor of the Chiado Department Stores, which had opened their doors a few weeks before.

THE DOLLS' HOSPITAL

The oldest dolls' hospital in Europe

Praça da Figueira, 7
Monday to Saturday, 10:30am–12:30pm and 3pm–5pm

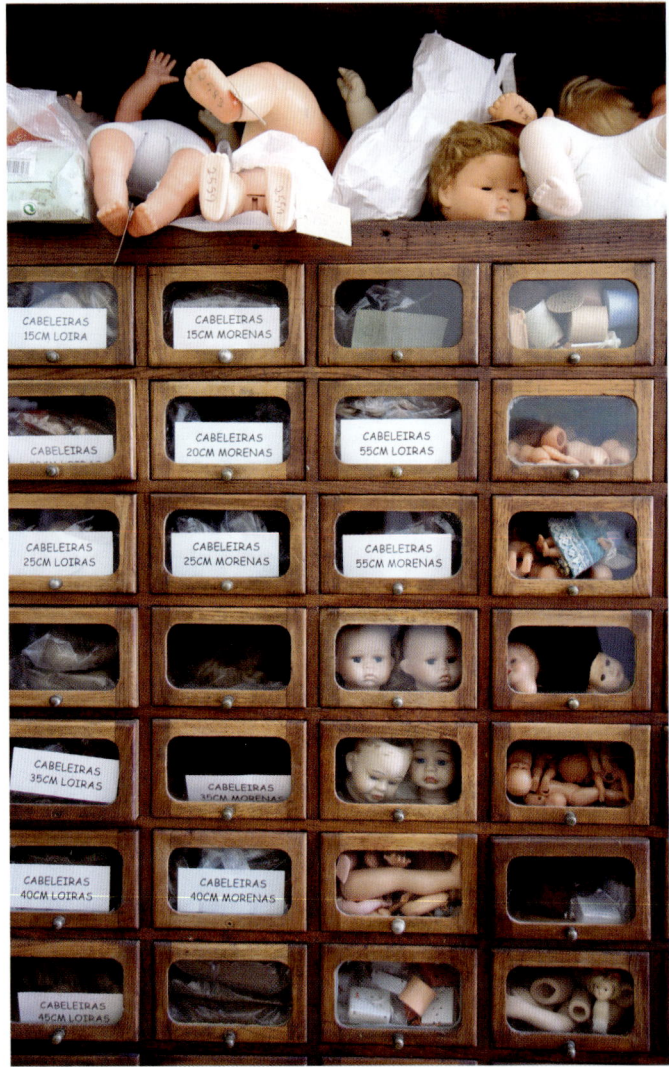

At No. 7 Praça da Figueira, in the centre of Lisbon's Baixa district, the Hospital das Bonecas (Dolls' Hospital) has been in business since 1830. Europe's oldest dolls' hospital, it is rather unique, as the dolls' hospitals of Madrid and London only repair valuable dolls, and that of New York is much more recent and provides fewer services. For almost 180 years, this hospital has continued to piece together the dreams of young children, the recollections of those who are no longer so young, and the memory of the past for all.

When dreams need repair, little ones, their parents and grandparents turn to the Hospital das Bonecas, through whose doors pass all sorts of sick or damaged dolls that sadden the imaginary world of their owners, especially children. All of them are treated with great care, from the old cardboard dolls made in Portugal until the 1960s, to Barbie dolls and McDonald's Happy Meal figurines.

The system of admission and treatment of the dolls is the same as in any hospital. When a patient arrives, his owner goes to the reception desk and fills out a form with a bed number that allows the hospital to identify the patients. Then, the dolls are placed on a stretcher, called *tinoni*, and are taken up the stairs to the workshop on the next floor. Each room is named according to the treatment provided. First, there is the plastic surgery room, where dolls are restored, repainted and given a new hairstyle. The trauma room is next door; it is for dolls that were the victims of games that were far too violent for their constitution. At the end of the hall you will find the transplant room full of legs, arms and heads of all styles and sizes, and next to this room is the morgue, where the doll doctors sometimes go to retrieve transplant parts. Finally, the residents' room is for dolls abandoned by their owners ...

When dolls become so damaged that they can no longer be fixed, their parts are donated to artists or, as has already been the case, to the Hospital da Estefânia, a specialised children's hospital that has been known to make paediatric prostheses from doll parts.

THE MEDALLION
OF TWO JOINED HANDS

Fraternal union between two squares

Corner of rua do Amparo
Metro Rossio

A few metres from Praça do Rossio and Praça da Figueira (Fig Tree square), at the corner of rua do Amparo (Mutual Aid street), a rather discreet medallion on the side of the building depicts two joined hands. A typical Masonic symbol, here it signifies the mutual aid between two squares.

This high relief was probably designed by Freemason architect Carlos Mardel who built Praça do Rossio and made it the central and vital pole of the city by moving the rural market that was once held there to the nearby Praça da Figueira. It was here that the main market was set up in 1755 after the ruins of the Todos os Santos hospital, which had burned down in 1750 and then collapsed in the earthquake, were cleared. This central market, which is now installed in an enclosed space in Art Nouveau style, had several successive names: *Horta do hospital* (Hospital vegetable garden), *Praça das Ervas* (Herbs square), *Praça Nova* (New square). In 1849, a wrought-iron fence with eight gates was installed around the already covered market. The square thus became one of the emblems of Pombaline Lisbon, thanks to its remarkable construction for the period and its importance as the true supply centre of the Baixa district.

Da Figueira, Rossio and Comércio squares became the three principle poles of the city's activities. The political or ministerial sector formed around Praça do Comércio, making it the centre of the country's political life, while the commercial or urban sector was centred on Rossio, with its countless shops and offices. And finally, rural life was focused on Figueira central market.

Thus, the two hands that join in a fraternal fashion unite Baixa's two squares and, through their traditional symbolism, express the union between the countryside and the city.

The Masonic salute

Freemasons salute each other by shaking hands in a distinctive manner. By pressing with their thumb, they indicate their rank. Using the tip of the thumb of the right hand, an apprentice will lightly touch the first knuckle of the other person's right index finger three times: two rapid touches and one long one. A companion will do the same, but will use his right thumb to touch the first knuckle of the other person's middle finger five times: two rapid touches, a long one, and two more rapid ones. A master will do likewise, but with seven touches: four rapid ones and three long ones.

PAINTING OF BOCAGE'S ARREST

'I'm Bocage, I've come from Café Nicola and I'll be in the next world if you fire that pistol'

Café Nicola, Praça do Rossio
Daily, 9am–11pm
Metro Rossio

Inside Café Nicola, one of the oldest literary cafés in town (it was mentioned in the *Gazeta de Lisboa* as early as 1787), a huge painting that dominates the room depicts a rather comical and memorable incident involving Bocage, the poet.

A billiard room was once connected to the café by a long corridor. Its entrance was at what is now No. 22 and 23 Praça do Rossio. This is the spot where Bocage was stopped by one of the chief of police Pina Manique's men who, aiming his pistol, asked: who are you, where have you come from, and where are you going? Bocage supposedly answered with a quatrain that has become famous, '*Eu sou o Bocage, venho do café Nicola e vou para o outro mundo se disparas a pistola*' ('I'm Bocage, I've come from Café Nicola and I'll be in the next world if you fire that pistol'). Was he under surveillance for his supposed Freemason membership, under

the pseudonym Lucrécio, from 1795 to 1797? Whatever the case, the incident was immortalised in the painting by Fernando Santos, who is also the artist responsible for the café's other paintings. Undoubtedly the primary representative of the 'Arcádia Lusitana' literary movement that he founded and popularised, Manuel Maria de Barbosa l'Hedois du Bocage (1765–1805) was a regular of Café Nicola. This is where he cursed his enemy, ex-priest Agostinho de Macedo, dictated his *Pena de Talião* (a satire about the latter) to a friend, and also where Nuno Pato Moniz wrote the comic poem *Agostinheida*, in which he ridiculed the famous priest for his dissolute lifestyle.

Bocage also recited improvised sonnets here, drawing a plethora of intellectuals and politicians. Even after the poet's death, his group of friends continued to meet at the café and organise literary gatherings. José Pedro da Silva, one of the café's waiters who had befriended the poets, helped them as best he could, notably by lending them enough money to make ends meet. He was even the person who paid for Bocage's burial.

Café Nicola closed in 1834 and did not reopen until 2 October 1929, when it adopted Bocage as its mascot. The facade, which also dates from 1929, was completed by Norte Júnior. Although the interior decor was originally neoclassic in style, architect Raul Tojal changed it to Art Deco style in 1935.

Café Nicola also has a statue of the poet on display, the work of sculptor Marcelino Norte d'Almeida.

Why is an espresso called a bica in Lisbon?

One legend claims that the name is derived from the acronym of an inscription displayed in the A Brasileira cafe: '*Beba Isto Com Açucar*' (Drink this with sugar), a recommendation said to have been written following complaints by clients who found their coffee too bitter. According to the current owner, the term *bica* does indeed originate with A Brasileira, but life was very different at the beginning of the 20th century, a period in which people strolled through the Chiado and luxuriated outside the bistrots. One day, the customers at A Brasileira complained, not about the bitterness but about the lack of taste. High-pressure machines had not yet come into existence and the filtered coffee was often prepared in advance. Served lukewarm on the day, it had lost its flavour on contact with the air. The manager at that time remade a coffee, which he then poured directly into the cups while hot, without transferring it into a coffee pot. The vessel in question had a tube (*bica*), which gave its name to the coffee being served.

THE SECRETS
OF TABACARIA MÓNACO

Forgotten objects for the benefit of smokers

Praça do Rossio, 21
Metro Rossio

Although it is well known to Lisbonites, the tobacconist's shop on Praça Dom Pedro IV (or Praça do Rossio) has three curios that few people notice.

Sitting in the middle of a long counter made of exotic wood, a 19th-century bronze cat keeps its true purpose concealed behind its motionless appearance. Only knowledgeable clients know that by simply operating its tail-guillotine, they are able to cut their cigars. Unfortunately for them, although the cat is still functioning, that is no longer the case with the nearby statuette of an old lady wearing a nightcap and holding a candle. Previously, this candle was permanently lit in order to allow smokers to light their cigars or cigarettes. Right beside them stands a stone washbasin on which are inscribed the names of three towns known for their spring water: Cintra, Caneças and Moura. This recalls an era when running water was not widely available and the tobacconist's shop provided this service.

The shop was opened with great pomp on 1 August 1894. The press of the time describes the presence of 4,000 onlookers who had come to admire, among other things, the azulejos by Rafael Bordalo Pinheiro exhibited in this unusual corridor-shop. In an obvious allusion to its commercial activities, the panels on the lower part of the left-hand wall show toads and herons smoking, handling snuff, reading newspapers of the period and drinking spring water. Painted by António Ramalho, the *trompe-l'œil* ceiling depicts swallows by the same ceramicist. The telegraph wires on which they are perched are a reminder of the public telephone kiosk that was previously located at the back of the shop.

As a plaque mounted next to the entrance by the first owner indicates, Tabacaria Mónaco is a place steeped in tradition.

The bust of Prince Albert I of Monaco

Prince Albert I of Monaco lent his name to the tobacconist's shop purely by chance during a visit to Lisbon at the beginning of the 20th century. In a fit of audacious zeal, the owner at the time swiftly renamed his store after the monarch. Positioned above the shelves, a bronze bust of the sovereign bears witness to this royal visit.

THE LAST VESTIGES
OF THE HOSPITAL
REAL DE TODOS OS SANTOS

*A hospital that occupied the site of the modern
Praça da Figueira*

Praça do Rossio, 85 – Metro Rossio

A t no. 85, Praça do Rossio, the imposing stone column occupying the window of a small clothes shop is one of the last vestiges of the All Saints Royal Hospital (*Hospital Real de Todos os Santos*), whose construction started in 1492 during the reign of João II.

The philanthropic sovereign wished to create a hospital providing care and medical assistance to the destitute in the heart of Lisbon. After João II's death, King Manuel I continued with the ambitious project, which was completed in 1504.

Paintings and engravings, as well as the azulejos panel (1740) displayed at the City Museum, allow us to see what Lisbon's most important medical facility between the 16th and 18th centuries looked like.

Built on the orchards of the São Domingos Convent, the building stood on the present-day Praça da Figueira. Supported by twenty-five arches, its 100-metre-long main facade faced Praça do Rossio, occupying its entire eastern side. In the centre, a monumental stairway gave access to the church, built in the Manueline style. Constructed over three levels, the cruciform building had 250 beds. A veritable model of innovation and ingenuity, it had emergency services, a pharmacy, an asylum for the mentally unbalanced, a paediatric department and (on payment of a fee) a private section for the nobility. The patients were divided according to sex and their particular pathology. They were given the absolute luxury of a cupboard for storing their personal possessions. The deceased were removed discreetly, using doors hidden behind each bed. A large altar, erected in the centre of the establishment, allowed residents to follow religious services from one of three symmetrical wings.

Damaged by fire in 1601 and 1750, the 'Great Hospital of the Poor' was destroyed by the earthquake of 1755. The sick and wounded were transferred to makeshift tents erected in the Praça do Rossio or to the palaces and monasteries that had been converted into temporary hospitals. Next to the shop where the stone column is found, a bureau de change displays a pho-tographic enlargement of an 18th-century engraving showing the Hospital Real de Todos os Santos in all its splendour. Behind the glass partition where the staff can be seen working, a fragment of its last arch is also visible.

THE PANELS
OF THE RESTORATION

The forgotten azulejos of the Independence

Gardens of the palace of the Counts of Almada
213 241 470
Guided tour by reservation on weekdays (minimum 5 people)
213 241 475
Metro Rossio

Located at the centre of Lisbon's Baixa quarter, near Praça do Rossio and São Domingos church, the Palace of the Restoration is known by several names: *Palácio des Condes de Almada* (Palace of the Counts of Almada), *da Restauração* (of the Restoration), or *da Independência* (of the Independence). When the patriotic revolt of 1 December 1640 took place, the palace's owner, Dom Antão de Almada, reunited here the 40 conspirators that gave Portugal back its independence after 60 years of Castilian rule. The conspirators met in secret in the palace gardens, which Dom Fernando de Almada, a captain of the Portuguese army, and his wife had bought from nobleman Dom Nuno de Barbudo in the 15th century. Upon entering the gardens, two large, cone-shaped brick towers can be seen on the roof (similar to the conical chimneys of the royal palace in Sintra) that Dom Antão de Almada had built and which illustrate the typical style of the Restoration period. Hardly touched by the earthquake of 1755 and relatively unknown to most Lisbon residents, the azulejo works called the *Panels of the Restoration* are located in the palace gardens. Dating from 1696, they are the work of Gabriel del Barco. One of them depicts the conspirators meeting here, in the gardens, as the title indicates: *Blessed place, honourable meetings where Portugal's Redemption was fulfilled*. Other panels show the victorious attack against the Spanish regents at the palace of Ribeira and the triumphal procession celebrating the Restoration.

In the garden, against the fernandina wall (from the period of King Dom Fernando in the 14th century) and to the right of the fountain and azulejo panels, lies another room where the conspirators' secret meetings were supposedly held. The participants descended the staircase in the fernandina wall, knocked on the door below, and, as a sort of password needed to gain entrance to the pavilion, showed a small silver tube that had a hidden spring at one end. Once activated, an image of Nossa Senhora da Conceição, the protector of Portugal, would appear.

When Christ blessed liberated Portugal

The fountain in the centre of the garden shows an angel below the words, *'Redemption of Portugal, Fidelity and Love triumph.'* This fountain represents the *Angel of Portugal Restored*, a theme based on the pious and patriotic legend that recounts that, during the procession celebrating the nation's independence, the Christ at the top of the crucifix held by Father Nicolau da Maia supposedly detached his right arm from the cross to bless the population and thus all of newly liberated Portugal.

PANORAMIC VIEW
OF LISBON

The last remaining picture of Lisbon before 1620

Church of Saint Louis of the French
Beco São Luis da Pena, 34
Daily, 9am–1pm
Metro and train Restauradores or Rossio

Inside the Church of Saint Louis of the French (*Saint-Louis des Français*), on the left-hand wall of the nave, hangs a painting commissioned by Captain Manhonet, a shipowner from Bordeaux. It is attributed to Domingos Vieira Serrão and Simão Rodrigues, both painters at the court of Philip III of Spain (who was also Philip II of Portugal). The painting gives the only view of Lisbon prior to 1620, many years before the 1755 earthquake. Providing unique historical evidence, the panoramic view encompasses Ribeira das Naus (the River of the Carracks) and the Jardim do Tabaco, revealing long-gone buildings and bringing the flourishing maritime and commercial activity of the period back to life. On the far left, four spires crowned with weather vanes cover the palace of the Corté Real family. Resold to the royal family, the palace was destroyed in 1755. In the left foreground, the four floors and dome of the graceful Terzi tower (c. 1590) suffered the same disastrous fate. The adjacent great square was used as a shipyard and delivery point for everyday goods (oil, wine, wood, fruit and even snow from the Serra da Estrela) and more exotic wares (such as spices, precious stones and silver) arriving from the East Indies.

In the foreground, the yellow-grey facades of the Terreiro do Paço (renamed Praça do Commercio at the end of the 18th century), painted

pink for the proclamation of the republic in 1910, have now been restored to their original saffron yellow. Nearby, a large esplanade hosted a market, overlooked by the Casa dos Bicos (1523). On the right-hand side, below São Jorge Castle, the Augustine Monastery of Our Lady of Grace is shown in its original state. On the Tagus, caravels, galleons from the Indies and frigates with billowing sails give a picture of intense maritime activity. In the clouds, the Virgin, surrounded by some twenty chubby cherubs, watches over the city. As a vignette located above, to the left, reminds us: 'Our Holy Lady of Safe Harbour prays to her precious Son on behalf of the city and its life on the river.' The painters of this ex-voto could never have imagined the tragedy that would befall Lisbon in 1755.

Opposite this view of Lisbon, there is a painting with a rare view of the streets of 17th-century Paris. The foreground of this remarkably life-like work tells the story of Saint Louis receiving the crown of thorns from the hands of Christ. On the right-hand side of the picture, the pulpit made of Lioz stone sitting on three devil heads symbolises the destruction of sin through preaching.

To the right of the choir, the infant Jesus was sculpted in Carrara marble by Elias Robert. He is also known as the creator of the monumental bronze statue of King Dom Pedro IV in the square of the same name.

The royal symbols found in the church (gilded, wooden fleurs-de-lys on the ceiling of the choir, royal escutcheon on the pulpit pediment, French coat of arms on the glacis of the windows overlooking the street) pay homage to Louis XV, who funded the reconstruction of the church in 1762, following the 1755 earthquake.

The National Tile [*Azulejo*] Museum (housed in the Convent of Madre de Deus) possesses a panel that also shows an interesting panorama of old Lisbon, although it only dates from 1725.

PÁTIO DO TRONCO TUNNEL

The place where Luís de Camões was arrested and sent to jail

Rua das Portas de Santo Antão, 13 – Metro Rossio

In among the theatres and popular restaurants along Rua das Portas de Santo Antão, an unattractive tunnel still succeeds in attracting the attention. On the walls, covered in brand-new azulejos made in 1992 by the ceramicist Leonel Moura, a gigantic 'Portugal Forever' stands out, written in white letters on a blue background. Written above, we find: 'On 16 June 1552, Luís Vaz de Camões was arrested near Santo Antão after being involved in a fight, and was then sent to the municipal prison of Tronco.' On the arch of the passage, the portrait of the great poet (1525–1580) – recognisable from his face with one damaged eye, the result of a brawl in Ceuta (Spain), where he had been exiled due to his escapades and repeated insolence – has been reproduced ten times.

While he was walking one evening in Rua das Portas de Santo Antão, the author of *Os Lusíades* (The Lusiads) was halted by the noise of a violent argument. On moving closer, the impetuous young man of 28 years saw two of his friends in difficulty. Without hesitation, he came to their aid and with a strike of his sword wounded one Gonçalo Borges, an aristocrat attached to the royal court, on the nape of the neck. Camões was imprisoned in the Tronco Prison, where he languished for nine long months, despite the pardon granted by the victim. He was forced to wait until 24 March 1553 before being liberated by royal letter. On the very same day, he embarked for the Indies, where he served as a soldier to make up for his previous offence. His stay in the penal institution left him with bitter memories mixed with humiliation, which he would later describe as follows:

In a lowly prison, I was for a time detained,
Shameful punishment for my errors;
Though today I am cast out, I still wear irons
Which only death, to my great regret, will break.

LIMA DE FREITAS' FIFTH EMPIRE PANELS

'Portugal has a lot to teach and bring to Europe'

Largo D. João da Câmara
Central Station of Rossio

In Rossio Station, 14 polychrome azulejo wall-panels are exhibited near the platforms. Produced by the Fábrica de Cerâmica de Constância in 1995-96 and based on models by Lima de Freitas (Setúbal, 1927 – Lisbon, 1998), these wall-panels are inspired by the myths and legends of Lisbon.

Initially influenced by neo-realism, Lima de Freitas quickly dedicated his work to the Portuguese imagery he drew and painted so skilfully, rather in the manner of Almada Negreiros, to whom he was close.

His murals filled with symbols notably depict the theories of the Fifth Empire (see p. 64), as the panel entitled *Vieira and the V Empire* so clearly illustrates.

The immense knowledge contained in these panels led Gilbert Durand, a personal friend of the artist, to declare, 'Portugal itself has many more myths than all of Europe put together, which could perhaps help the latter realise its destiny.'

Sª Auta diante da Madre de Deus

The following words from Lima de Freitas seem to echo Durand: 'Portugal has no reason to feel ashamed with regard to the rest of Europe.

On the contrary, we have a lot to teach and bring to it. The Mission that concerns our principal qualities – our deeply-rooted sense of human brotherhood, the idea of Universality, and the vision of the Fifth Empire.'

A fifteenth panel by the same artist can be seen in the Restauradores metro station, which is directly connected to the central station.

TUDO O QUE ABRAÇA O MAR
TUDO O QUE ALUMIA O SOL...
SERÁ SUJEITO A ESTE QUINTO IMPÉRIO...
TODAS AS COROAS SE REMATARÃO
EM UM SÓ DIADEMA
E ESTE SERÁ A PEANHA
DA CRUZ DE CRISTO

HISTÓRIA DO FUTURO, CAP. III

· VIEIRA · E · O · V · IMPÉRIO ·

Fez te mercê, barão, a Sapiência Suprema de c'ós olhos corporais Vejas o que não pode a...

ciência

...dos errados e míseros mortais

A visão cósmica de Camões

LVSIADAS

Vês aqui a grande máquina do Mundo

X. 80

SECRET PASSAGE
OF THE AVENIDA PALACE HOTEL

16

Spies at Avenida Palace

Rua Primeiro de Dezembro, 123
Metro Restauradores

A lthough Portugal remained neutral during the Second World War, the Avenida Palace hotel was a nest of German, British and American spies. The hotel's employees tell incredible stories about this period and show interested visitors some of the secret passages used by the spies.

The hotel was so notorious for this reason that Lisbon is even mentioned in the film *Casablanca*.

On the fourth floor, a mysterious door leading to another door that has been locked since 1955 can still be seen. Behind it, a corridor connects the hotel to Rossio station, which allowed VIPs and spies arriving under diplomatic cover to arrive incognito and evade police controls.

One legendary spy was known by the code name *Garbo*. A Spanish citizen living in Lisbon, this spy gave the Germans false information fabricated from simple geography books about the British way of life. Thanks to him, the Germans came to believe that they had lost the aerial war with Britain, although that was not necessarily the case. This all happened in the period before the Allied invasion of Europe when rumours circulated about the possible landing sites: Normandy or the Pas-de-Calais, which was the more likely option given its proximity to Britain.

Considered to be the most luxurious hotel of the Baixa district, the Avenida Palace was founded on 10 October 1892 by the *Wagons-lits* tourism company, based in Paris. Architect Luís Monteiro was in charge of the project aimed at European tourists arriving in Lisbon at Rossio station. The hotel has 82 rooms and 20 suites, a large lounge, a Belle Époque restaurant and an Empire-style dining room.

The hotel's illustrious guests have included Emperor Hirohito of Japan, who spent his honeymoon here, banker Alves dos Reis, admiral Américo Thomaz and the Portuguese president Sidónio Pais, who was assassinated on his way to the hotel.

THE SECRETS OF
THE DOM SEBASTIÃO STATUE

17, Portugal's key number

Largo D. João da Câmara
Central Station of Rossio

At the centre of Rossio station's main facade, at the point where two horseshoe-shaped arches meet, stands a statue of Dom Sebastião, the king who perished in the battle of Alcazarquivir (Arabic *Ksar el-Kebir*, Battle of the Three Kings) in North Africa, 1578.

As Rossio central is a place of waiting and of hope, there is no better place for this departed king who determined Portugal's fatal destiny. As a result of his defeat, the country fell under the rule of Castile, thus losing its independence for 60 years.

The number 17 can be found everywhere on this facade. The king is shown at the young age of 17. He is dressed in period clothing, bears his royal insignia on his chest, and holds a shield sporting Portugal's coat of arms in front of him at an angle of 17°. Note that 17 is also the total sum of the facade's eight doors and nine windows. In addition, the number 17 refers to Portugal's 'biorhythm' as its history seems to unfold in 17-year cycles (see p. 98). The king holds his sword in front of his shield; his hands seem to hide two castles, leaving five visible, a symbolic reference to the Fifth Empire tradition elaborated in Lisbon and imagined at Sintra (see p. 64). In the facade's two horseshoe-shaped arches, one can also see the horseshoes of the white horse on which the Secret King is supposed to arrive one misty morning, as prophesised by the Portuguese Sebastianic utopia – a prophesy with which the statue's sculptor, Simões de Almeida, was probably familiar. Almeida had already sculpted a plaster model of Dom Sebastião when he was crown prince (1874), a work he later created in marble, in 1878, and which figured in the Paris World's Fair.

This building's exuberant neo-Manueline style exterior was designed by architect José Luís Monteiro in partnership with Adães Bermudes. Built in 1886-87, the station was opened on 23 November 1890 and was called the *Estação Avenida*. It was an audacious accomplishment for the period, since it applied an architectural style and aesthetic movement that had only been used for royal, noble or other official edifices to a public railway station.

On 14 December 1918, another king-president, Sidónio Pais, was assassinated at the foot of this statue. At the time, many people acclaimed Pais as a reincarnation of Dom Sebastião. Perhaps it was for that reason that he was assassinated.

17, Portugal's key number

Several authors justify Portugal's special mission by referring to the following verse from the Bible: 'I have set thee to be a light [Lux] of the Gentiles [*Citânia*], that thou shouldest be for salvation unto the ends of the earth' (Acts 13:47). They also refer to the salutary role of the arcanum 17 in tarot – Hope, a card that bears the name Star. The miracle of the battle of Ourique (25 July 1139, Saint James Day, according to the Chronicle of the Goths) seems to have confirmed this mission. During the famous battle, Christ supposedly appeared to Dom Afonso Henriques and assured him that he would renew the Portuguese nation in the sixteenth generation to follow him (which corresponds to Dom Sebastião). We should note that sixteen generations, plus the original generation, makes 17 generations.

In tarot, the number 17 is the Star, which indicates 'that which is secret must be revealed', in accordance with the etymological meaning of the term *Apocalypse*. Furthermore, adding the 1 and the 7 of 17 gives the number 8, which, in tarot, corresponds to the card of Justice, represented by the Archangel Michael, and which is adapted from the celebrated saying 'you are born in Portugal either with a mission or as a punishment'. In other words, those born in Portugal either

serve humanity or suffer with it, meaning that the two extremes are one and the same. In his horoscope of Portugal, Fernando Pessoa (see p. 61) begins with the year 1128 (24 June, the date of the battle of São Mamade between Dom Afonso Henriques and his mother Dona Teresa) and ends with 1978. It is interesting to note that the period covered is 850 years, or exactly 50 cycles of 17 years. From 1877 to 1978, Portugal would go through a lunar (punishment) cycle, with the period after 1978 marking the beginning of a new global solar cycle that would create the conditions necessary for Portugal to carry out its world mission in full. Astrologically, Pessoa links Portugal's entrance into the 'Fifth

House of the Sun' to the five wounds of Christ (which themselves are related to the five shields on the Portuguese flag) and to the idea of the Fifth Empire (see p. 64) ruling over the entire world from Lisbon. The number 17 is also the exact number of streets in the Baixa Pombalina district, as well as the number of figures depicted in the central panel of Nuno Gonçalves' polyptych (see p. 170). Nor should we forget the national standard, which used to be displayed at an inclination of 17° to the right and was not set upright until the reign of Dom João II. You can see the coat of arms displayed in its original form on the statue of Dom Sebastião at the entrance to Rossio central station (see p. 96).

Why was Portugal's coat of arms straightened?

Dom João II (1455-1495), thirteenth king of Portugal, was nicknamed the *Perfect Prince* for his authoritarian and Machiavellian exercise of power. During his reign, he took constant reprisals against the nobility who opposed his absolutism. He suppressed the municipal councils and dispossessed the Order of Christ, the main force of resistance, and even went so far as to have his administrator, Dom Diogo, duke of Viseu, assassinated in 1484. The duke was stabbed in the back in the palace of Setubal. In 1485, the king ordered that all the insignias of the Order of Christ be removed from the caravels. He had already had those of the House of Avis eliminated and replaced by royal emblems identifying no specific group, thus considerably weakening the national spirit.

Understanding nothing of the symbolism of the Portuguese coat of arms, Dom João II had the shields of Portugal's armorial bearings modified with the so-called 'Operation to straighten the coat of arms' carried out in the same year. To the nobility who tried to oppose the change, he responded with the famous phrase, 'I am the lord of lords, not the serf of serfs'.

Dom Sebastião, the 'chimerical king'

Dom Sebastião I (Lisbon, 20 January 1554 – Alcazarquivir, Morocco, 4 August 1578) was the sixteenth king of Portugal and the seventh of the Avis dynasty. He was the son of Prince Dom João, who himself was the son of Dom João III and Dona Joana, the daughter of Holy Roman emperor Charles V. Dom Sebastião left no descendants. Dom Sebastião became heir to the throne at the death of his father, two weeks before his birth. He became king in 1557, at the age of three. The long-awaited heir of the Avis dynasty, he was known as *The Desired One*, *The Hidden One*, or *The Dormant King* (a sort of Messiah) because of the legend telling of his return one misty morning to save the nation (see p. 123).

Dom Sebastião's tutor, Jesuit father Luís Gonçalves da Câmara, made of him a visionary monk, while his riding instructor, Dom Aleixo de Menezes, turned him into a passionate horseman. These two threads to his education, particularly the first, made of Dom Sebastião an accomplished military monk, a Roman Catholic who fanatically opposed heresy and a man exalted at the idea that Portugal would dominate the world. The stage was set for the tragedy that would ruin the country.

The chivalric ideal conceived by Dom Sebastião pushed him to devour the works of this literary genre, to turn over the tombs of his ancestors at the monastery of Batalha in search of who knows what, in his frenzied desire for military feats surpassing those of previous kings. His religious ideal made of him a Puritan, a feigned ascetic who dreamed of running through the Sintra mountains and finding a 'Grail'.

At the age of 14, Dom Sebastião took over the governing of the Empire. Of fragile health and simple of mind, he dreamed only of battles, conquests and spreading the Faith. Consecrating little time to the affairs of his vast empire, he was profoundly convinced that he would be Christ's captain in a crusade against the Moors of North Africa and would conquer Jerusalem, where he would become 'King of the World'. Dominated by his dreams of glory, he ignored the sensible advice of his wisest councillors and, in his madness, went off to lose himself, and Portugal along with him, in the midst of the African sands of Ksar el-Kebir (Alcazarquivir). He was 24 years old. The unfortunate young king's uncle, Filipe II of Spain, occupied Portugal, politically and militarily subjugating it to Castilian rule; the nation's independence was lost. Soon, patriotic hopes that the lost Dom Sebastião would return to deliver the country from its Spanish occupiers arose, thus giving rise to the Sebastianist myth of *The Hidden One* (see p. 64).

To put an end to the development of Sebastianism, Filipe II had the supposed body of the lost king transported to the monastery of the Hieronymites in 1581, but this did not help in the least as there was no proof that it was indeed the lost king. And yet, engraved on the tomb were the words, 'Dom Sebastião, king of Portugal and of everything else', meaning the world.

THE UNDERGROUND ABBEY
OF PALÁCIO FOZ

A secret underground abbey

Palácio Foz, Praça dos Restauradores
Visits by appointment by calling 213 221 215 or 213 221 362 (currently closed for redevelopment – expected to reopen in 2025)

S till today, an extraordinary 'abbey', a former restaurant where secret meetings were held up to the 1940s, lies beneath the Palácio Foz.

It is divided into three sections: the *claustrum* (cloister) with its *taverna vínica* (wine tavern) as the distich indicates, the *refectorium* (refectory) inspired by the Roman Cistercian cloisters of the Iberian Peninsula, and the *coro* (choir) that overhangs the refectory and leads to the cells.

This restaurant was almost exclusively reserved for the Masonic elite (men and women of the Ancient and Accepted Scottish Rite of Freemasonry) as well as for the elite members of the *Club dos Makavenkos*, a bohemian society that organised banquets and whose members, for the most part, were connected to Masonic humanism.

The site is entirely based on esoteric symbolism (Masonic, Kabbalistic and theosophic) and is inspired by Lusitanian myths. The Masonic presence cannot be denied as 24 small busts of Freemasons, both men and women, some of whom bear the insignia of their rank on their chest, line the *refectorium*'s north and south walls.

Also seen there is a strange, mythic figure (a dragon-woman), doves and swallows in relief in the corners of the room, ship rudders bearing the effigies of Vasco da Gama and Pedro Álvares Cabral, the hanging statue of a medieval architect, a beautiful coral fountain next to a well leading to underground Lisbon, and a small balcony decorated with ropes, pulleys and a fisherman's knot, underneath, in relief. Red marble Tuscan columns and green marble colonnades further enliven this place reserved for the secret meetings and agapes of Lisbon's Freemasons.

The Palácio Foz, which was the largest residence in Lisbon until the end of the 19th century, was owned by the marquis of Castelo Melhor who had it built in 1777, following a design by Italian architect Francisco Xavier Fabri.

Later, in 1889, the Castelo Melhor family sold the palace to financier Tristão Guedes de Queirós Correia Castelo Branco, the second count and first marquis of Foz.

In April 1917, the *pastelaria* Foz (Foz pastry shop), which occupied several rooms on the ground floor as well as the cellar, opened its doors. In the cellar, an Art Nouveau restaurant, the *Abadia* (Abbey), was launched in a blend of neo-Gothic and neo-Manueline styles.

Freemason agapes

Modern Freemasonry inherited the agapes (also called banquets) tradition, which was popularised in Portugal during the Napoleonic wars, from the Judaeo-Christian tradition. In their purest sense, the agapes are Popular Feasts of the Empire of the Divine Holy Spirit, where everyone, regardless of social class, shared the same table for the *bodo* (meal), after the mass. Of Portuguese origin, these feasts were celebrated in Alfama and São Sebastião da Pedreira.

Agapes is Greek for *love feast*. The early Christians celebrated this feast as illustrations of friendship, love and mutual benevolence. These charity banquets were begun in Rome by Saint Clement during the reign of Domitian (1st century) and come from a tradition directly inherited from the Mysteries of the Sun god Mitra that Christianity adapted in the episode of the Last Supper of Jesus Christ (see our guide *Secret Rome*).

The early Christians celebrated these fraternal banquets before they celebrated Eucharistic communion. Composed of various dishes, and not simply bread and wine, they were presided over by apostles, then later by bishops and priests. From the 3rd century, the agapes had a tendency to degenerate into orgies, to the point that the Church abolished them when a bishop could no longer control them.

In the 18th century, the Masonic tradition reclaimed the hierarchical organisation and traditions of early Christianity, including the ritual agapes, which are directly connected to the meals or banquets of Masonic lodges. Nevertheless, the *santo beijo* (holy kiss) and women were excluded from them, and the banquets became more like 'drinking' feasts than 'love' feasts.

The love feast survives in the Eucharist, the central part of the mass when the priest raises up and consecrates the bread and wine, which thus become living parts of the body of God.

The symbols of Palácio Foz's Abadia

In the former *Abadia* (Abbey) restaurant in the cellar of Palácio Foz stands a curious full-size sculpture of a medieval architect. Wearing a Phrygian cap and supporting a column displaying two elephant heads with intertwined trunks, he represents the Grand Architect of the Temple of Virtue and Wisdom. The elephants represent the temple (one designates the wisdom of the spirit and the other the virtue of the soul). A Hindu icon of the god Ganesh, son of Shiva, the elephant is the patron of the Gupta Vidya or secret Wisdom. Since he holds the secrets of the Royal Art (Geometry and Mathematics), the Master Architect is the keeper of wisdom and virtue. He is believed to be the perfect illustration of the Royal Follower or Perfect Man, keeper of the Sacerdotal Art, and builder of churches, cathedrals, palaces and castles throughout Europe. Beneath the sculpture, a well is believed to descend into the bowels of Lisbon. To the right, a beautiful coral fountain symbolically represents the *fons de Sé* (fountain of Wisdom), from which the *Acqua Vitae* flows. This water purifies the body and inspires the soul of he who becomes the perfect Follower, as personified by the Grand Architect.

Bairro Alto, Santa Catarina, Chiado, Campo Santana

THE *AZULEJOS* OF THE CARDAES CONVENT ①

A little-known wonder

Cardaes Convent
Rua de O Século, 123
Monday to Saturday, 2:30pm–5pm
Tram 24E

F ew Lisbon residents know the wonderful Convent of Nossa Senhora da Conceição dos Cardaes (Our Lady of Conception), or simply the Convent of Cardaes, which was built between 1681 and 1703 under the auspices of its founder, Dona Luísa de Távora. Its church, which consists of a single nave, is decorated with paintings and azulejo panels by the Dutch artist Jan Van Oort illustrating the life of St. Teresa de Ávila. Its vast collection of 18th-century azulejos and azujelos known as '*joaninos*' is unique in Lisbon.

The convent consists of a church, two cloisters, a refectory and several outbuildings. The larger cloister, which overlooks the garden and is paved with tombstones, has walls covered in china and a small stone washbasin in the centre. In the rectangular-shaped refectory, the azulejo decoration is of blue and white *albarradas* and *padrão camellias*. In the church, the main altar is made of sculpted wood, decorated with a thin layer of gold, and forms a sort of enclosed compartment thanks to the painting depicting the *Immaculate Conception with St. John of the Cross and other Carmelite Saints*, executed by the painter André Gonçalves from a drawing by Vieira Lusitano.

In 1834, following the publication of the law on the suppression of the religious orders, the liberal regime decided to close the convent on the death of its last resident. However, before her death, the institution changed its name, becoming 'The Association [of Our Mother] Protector of the Afflicted [of the Sisters of the Third Order of St. Dominic]', thus bypassing the decree and its prohibition. A group of believing Catholics signed a petition prior to the death of the last sister in March 1876. The document, which was remarkably well phrased and argued, requested permission from the state to convert the convent into a charity and to preserve the devotional and liturgical items. In order to prevent the building from falling into ruin, the former Cardaes Convent of Jesus, its enclosure, church and goods were assigned to the charity and it was used as a home for blind invalids. In 1878, the convent was given to the Sisters of the Third Order of St. Dominic. It remains in their possession today.

From Portuguese azulejos to Dutch ceramics

The upper portion of the choir, which is attached to the church, has an imposing iron grid and azulejo panels depicting scenes from the life of St. Teresa, which appear to complement the panels created by Jan Van Oort visible on the ground floor. It is amusing to note the ubiquitous deep blue of the Portuguese tiles contrasted with the dominant white of the Flemish versions.

THE SCULPTURE OF ADAMASTOR ②

A symbol of the superstitions of certain Sebastianists

Belvedere of Alto de Santa Catarina
Tram 28E

At Alto de Santa Catarina stands a strange sculpture by Júlio Vaz Júnior dating from 1927, the meaning of which is often forgotten today. The statue depicts *Adamastor*, a monstrous mythical figure imagined by Luís de Camões in his work *Os Lusíadas*. Adamastor was a terrifying sea god who lived near Cape Boujdour, on the African coast, and who swallowed up the ships that came near him. He was thus a kind of ogre used by the Portuguese naval fleet in the 15th century to keep the superstitious ships of other countries from following them on the maritime routes they used and that only they knew. In *Mensagem*, Fernando Pessoa called him *Mostrengo* (Great Monster).

Santa Catarina: a belvedere for the lost

'Watch the ships from the top of Santa Catarina' is a popular 19th-century Portuguese expression dating from 1807. During the French invasions, the demoralised people stood on the heights of Santa Catarina to watch the ships carrying the royal family leave the Tagus estuary, on their way to the Brazilian royal court. The country thus abandoned and left to despair, only one solution remained: turn towards the Bandarra prophecies that the highly respected Father António Vieira had popularised. It was at this time that Alto de Santa Catarina, near Calçada do Combro, became a curious hideout for lost Sebastianists (see p. 122) who gathered, in a sort of urban 'new age' movement, without judgment or organisation, equipped with telescopes pointed at the estuary, hoping to see the arrival of the ship of the long-awaited King Dom Sebastião. They did not know if he would arrive from Africa, Brazil, or some unknown island hidden in the ocean ... and this tradition has survived, not largely followed, but still alive. This is the origin of red Sebastianism, better known as royal millenarianism, a political trend based on all sorts of prophecies and that sees symbols and signs in everything that is social and immediate, with much incoherence and ridicule. There is also white Sebastianism, which is completely different, being enlightened and holding metaphysical meaning. Although more coherent, it is the lesser-known aspect of Portuguese millenarianism (see p. 123).

CAGLIOSTRO AT PALÁCIO SOBRAL

The place where Mozart's 'Magic Flute' was played for Cagliostro

Largo do Calhariz, beginning of Calçada do Combro – Tram 28E

The fact that Alessandro Cagliostro, Count of Fénix (see opposite), spent time in Lisbon is largely unknown. However, Cagliostro played a determining role in Portuguese Freemasonry. After a journey from Rome to Santiago de Compostela, Cagliostro arrived in Lisbon on 25 April 1787, accompanied by his wife, Serafina Feliciani. They lodged at the Café Central in rua de Remolares on the cais do Sodré. After receiving an invitation from the Sobrais brothers, the couple took up residence at the Palácio Sobral, which Joaquim Inácio da Cruz Sobral had acquired after making his fortune in Salvador da Bahia, Brazil, thanks to his brother José Francisco da Cruz, who had introduced him to business affairs. The Sobral family also had close connections with the Marquis of Pombal. The parties and literary salons at Palácio Sobral were

memorable. It was in this enlightened milieu that Cagliostro made his entrance. A few months later, in 1788, the illustrious Count of Saint-Germain, a Rosicrucian Grand Master, and his wife Lorenza Feliciani also arrived in Lisbon with a delegation from the embassy of Venice. It was in this palace that Cagliostro and Serafina initiated Joaquim Inácio da Cruz Sobral and his sister, Ana Joaquina da Cunha Sobral, into the mysteries of Egyptian Freemasonry. On 2 August 1887, the palace was finally sold by its last private owner, the Marquis of Sousa Holstein, to the *Caixa Geral de Depósitos* (a state-owned banking corporation). No sooner had the transaction taken place than a fire broke out, almost destroying the entire premises, which is why the bank did not move in until 15 February 1947, after a complete renovation.

Cagliostro, an occultist who inspired Mozart, Goethe and Alexandre Dumas

A master of the occult arts and sciences, alchemist and therapist, Alessandro Cagliostro was born in Palermo in 1743 and died in Rome in 1795. He is generally associated with Giuseppe Balsamo, an individual about whom little is known, besides the fact that he was a traveller and alchemist who had spent his childhood at the monastery of Caltagirone, in Sicily. Alessandro Cagliostro is believed to have been raised by the Tavernays, a noble French family. His biological father, Cardinal Emmanuel of Rohan, Master of the Order of Malta, supposedly conceived him during a moment of weakness with the Marquise of Tavernay, but he abandoned the child. During his childhood, Cagliostro was apparently taken to Egypt and educated in a monastery of the Coptic Church; he was thus in contact with the monastery's spiritual Masters. From there, he is believed to have travelled to India and Tibet. On his way back to Europe, he visited the Middle East: Egypt, Arabia, Persia, Rhodes and Malta. In Messina or Rhodes, he supposedly met the Count of Saint-Germain, who initiated him in the mysteries of the hermetic tradition. In Malta, he was regularly seen at the court of Manuel Pinto, a native of Portugal and the new Grand Master of the Military Order of the Knights of Saint John of Malta. Thanks to Maltese influence, he made his first appearance in Rome as a count and frequented the noblest Italian families. There, he met Serafina Feliciani, who later became his wife. In 1772, Cagliostro and his wife settled in France. They were known to be benefactors for the poor, therapists for the needy and prodigious Masters of the Holy Science. In Lyon, Cagliostro founded the first Lodge of his so-called Egyptian Freemasonry (androgynous or Coptic), and popularised it throughout France, England, Germany, Holland, Poland and Russia, with phenomenal success, thanks to his great charisma and vast knowledge of occult sciences. These attributes gained him entrance to all the European courts and, in particular, that of French King Louis XVI. Cagliostro warned the king of the Revolution that was about to break out and of the danger threatening the royal family. In 1785, he was involved in Queen Marie-Antoinette's famous 'diamond necklace affair'. Accused of stealing the necklace, he was imprisoned in the Bastille, where he wrote his memoirs. The Parisian police eventually proved Cagliostro's innocence and he was freed. In Rome, The Inquisition imprisoned him for heresy in 1789. Condemned to death in 1791, his sentence was commuted to life imprisonment at the castle of San Leo. It is said that he died there from disease and poor medical treatment in 1795. Yet it is also claimed that he was secretly removed from the prison and sent to North America, along with his wife. As regards her fate, it is said that she was also condemned to reclusion for life in a religious convent, but these claims are found only in Jesuit documents. Along with the Count of Saint-Germain, Alessandro Cagliostro was one of the most extraordinary figures of the 18th century, so extraordinary, in fact, that Mozart dedicated his work *The Magic Flute* (1768) to him, Goethe used his life as inspiration for his drama *Der Grosskophta* (1792), and Alexandre Dumas made him the hero of his novel *Memoirs of a Physician* (1846).

Egyptian mysteries revealed in The Magic Flute

It was in the luxurious rooms of Palácio Sobral that Mozart's *Magic Flute* was played for the first time in Portugal, around 1793. Mozart had dedicated the work to his master Sarastro, referring to Cagliostro who had formerly spent some time there.

The name *Sarastro* means 'fifth star' (Venus) and it figures in the opera's libretto with the same spelling, just like the name Hierophant, taken from the Egyptian mysteries that this work transposes into music in brilliant fashion.

Wolfgang Amadeus Mozart received his initiatory knowledge from Cagliostro in person, after being initiated into the 'Charity' Masonic Lodge of Vienna, Austria, on 14 December 1784.

The premiere of *The Magic Flute* took place on 30 September 1791, also in Vienna.

PALÁCIO DO MANTEIGUEIRO

A miser's hidden splendours

Rua da Horta Seca, 15
Visits sometimes possible on request
Metro Baixa-Chiado

The Palácio do Manteigueiro (Butter Merchant's Palace), or Palácio Condeixa, where the Ministry of Energy is now located, is connected to rua das Chagas (Wounds street) by a gate giving access to a passage leading to the garden behind the building.

Originally, the palace only had one floor with a sloping roof, and two other ground-floor wings on the side facing rua da Emenda, due to the slope. The three upper floors were added later. On the exterior, note the stonework of the balcony windows of the second floor; the central window bears the coat of arms of the Viscount of Condeixa. Also note the main gate, the courtyard, the square paved with black and white marble stones, as well as the main staircase, quite remarkable despite having been stripped of its former ornamentation, and the chapel on the second floor displaying magnificent sculpted wood and a beautiful dome.

The interior was impressively elegant. The doors of Brazilian wood were covered in damask and the ceilings painted by Pedro Alexandrino (1730-1810). The crystal mirrors were framed in pure gold 'obtained by melting gold objects'.

Manuel Caetano de Sousa seems to have been behind the project for this palace, which dates back to 1787 and was built by Domingos Mendes Dias, a native of the Trás-os-Montes region.

Domingos Mendes Dias, a true miser

Domingos Mendes Dias was a curious man. After running away from his parents' home to come to Lisbon, he worked as a water carrier and apprentice salesman. Involved in dubious affairs relating to the expulsion of Jesuits from the kingdom, he ended up quite rich. After the earthquake of 1755, he emigrated to Brazil where he increased his wealth and even obtained a noble title. The palace's name came from his business of selling butter in bulk. An extremely rich man, Domingos Mendes Dias was a true miser. He lived alone with an old female servant. It is said that he had his dinner served in the drawer of his writing desk so that he could close it if an unexpected visitor arrived. His greatest pleasure was 'making up cartons of one hundred gold coins'. Refusing to spend money on medicine, he died of gangrene in his own bed, having been stabbed during an attempted robbery. At his death in 1836, the palace became the headquarters of the *Assembleia Lisbonense* of the partisans of the *Carta constitucional* (Constitutional Charter).

TOMBS OF THE SEBASTIANISTS ⑤

Mystics who believed in the return of King Sebastian

São Roque church – Largo Trindade Coelho – Metro Baixa-Chiado – Tram 24E
Monday to Saturday, 10am–6pm

Built at the end of the 16th century based on plans drawn up by architect Felipe Terzi for the site of the hermitage of the same name, the monumental São Roque (Saint Roch) church was granted to the Jesuits by Dom João III. This church of impressive artistic splendour was strongly marked in the past by the presence of the inspired Sebastianists, a blend of prophets, visionaries and saints, as the miraculous relics venerated in the side altar demonstrate. Some inspired Jesuits also propagated millenarian myths, including Father António Vieira who preached in this very place his famous *Sermão das 40 horas* (40-hour sermon), revealing part of his theories regarding the Fifth Empire (see p. 64). In the 16th and 17th centuries, numerous 'prophet cobblers' appeared. Nicknamed the *bandarra*, they were endowed with the gift of prophecy for the past, present and future. One of them, Simão Gomes, is buried in the church in front of the altar to the Virgin. At the time of Dom Sebastião, when he was a member of the Council of State, he poured out inspired prophecies that, when put into practice, were of great political use. He died in a state of grace in October 1576. The grave of another Sebastianist, Dom Francisco Tregian, can be found half-way along the left side of the building. This Englishman, who was reputed for his great saintliness, died on 25 December 1608. He had adopted Lisbon as his new home at a young age.

The spiritual vocation of these individuals is perfectly reflected in Saint Roch, who is described as a pilgrim whose knee is visible and who is accompanied by a dog. The pilgrim is the image of someone searching for knowledge by following the initiatory path of knowledge that he discovers step by step. The dog is the animal of the wise man, the follower's companion who protects him on the path of his choice. The uncovered left knee is the unequivocal sign of initiation, an initiation that is often identified with the circle of the compass that is used to trace the plans of the house of God.

Fado: *Portuguese identity linked to sebastianism?*

In his philosophical theories, Fernando Pessoa united the elements of theosophy and the idea of Destiny, or *fado* (*fatum* in Latin), to make Messianic Sebastianism a unique characteristic of Portuguese cultural identity.

Sebastianism and messianism

Strictly speaking, Messianism is the prophetic belief of the universal coming or return of a holy liberator, a Messiah (*Mashiah* in Hebrew, *Christos* in Greek, *Avatara* in Hindu). Sebastianism is a mystic movement that appears patriotic and grew during the second half of the 16th century following the death of King Dom Sebastião at the battle of Ksar el-Kebir in 1578 (see p. 100). As he had no heir, the Portuguese throne fell into the hands of King Felipe II, of the Spanish branch of the Habsburg family. Sebastianism is an Iberian form of Messianism adapted to this situation that was dramatic for the Portuguese. This tradition expresses their refusal of the established political situation and their hope for a way out, undoubtedly a miraculous one. According to common belief, the king was simply hidden (*encoberto*), waiting somewhere for the right time to return to Portugal, take back his throne and push out the occupying Spanish forces. The most popular propagator of Sebastianism was the cobbler of the city of Trancoso, Gonçalo Anes, nicknamed *Bandarra* (1500-1556), who predicted the return of the *Desired King* (as Dom Sebastião was also called) in popular verse. The main intellectual figure adhering to the movement was, nevertheless, Father António Vieira (1608-1697) (see p. 66), who developed the theme in depth. Portuguese poet Fernando Pessoa (1888-1935), in his book of patriotic poems entitled *Mensagem*, also provided a reinterpretation and eulogy of the history of Portugal enlightened by Sebastianism, thus aiming to unite the country's historic past to its spiritual future. Sebastianism, the belief of the return of the lost Dom Sebastião, was thus linked to the already existing Messianism by adding the hagiography of Saint Sebastian the martyr.

Messianism and the Fifth Empire

Some empower the Messiah in a much wider way, believing he is destined for all humanity and to inaugurate a new evolutionary cycle on a planetary scale. He will manifest himself by attitudes resulting from the feeling of being 'elected' or 'called' to accomplish a 'holy' task. During the reign of Dom João V, this led to the distinction between the new Patriarchal church of Lisbon, which represented the future, and the old Episcopal church of Rome, representing the past. Here, we find the theme of the *translatio imperii* with the future Fifth Empire (see p. 64).

THE SEVEN PAINTINGS ON THE ALTAR OF THE CHURCH OF SÃO ROQUE

A painting that is changed 7 times a year!

São Roque church – Largo Trindade Coelho
Monday to Saturday, 10am–6pm
Metro Baixa-Chiado – Tram 24E

It's a wonderful secret that the main painting above the church's altar is changed seven times a year to match the liturgical calendar.

Thus, seven different paintings follow one another in the same place: for the Annunciation, for the birth of Jesus at Christmas (adoration of the Magi), for the circumcision of Jesus (January), for Easter (for Calvary and the crucifixion, then the resurrection – two paintings), for Pentecost

(when the apostles receive the Holy Spirit and, in particular, the gift of tongues) and for the Assumption of the Virgin (Mary's ascent into Heaven). It is the painting of the circumcision that remains out of these liturgical times.

The first five paintings come from Seville and were painted in 1633 (author unknown) and the other two (Calvary and Annunciation) were added around 1680 (they are attributed to Bento Coelho da Silveira).

The cycle of seven paintings and the Spiritual Exercises of Saint Ignatius of Loyola

According to an interesting analysis in the book *Sete imagens para o Calendário Litúrgico* (in Portuguese and English, available from the church shop), the cycle of seven paintings at São Roque was not just a 'Bible for the illiterate', according to Gregory the Great's concept of religious paintings.

It would have been designed in conjunction with the Spiritual Exercises of Saint Ignatius of Loyola, to provide a visual reminder of the spiritual teaching associated with the image in question. The highly original way in which the paintings are rotated allows for dynamic mental prayer throughout the year.

The circumcision of Jesus: the first time Jesus shed his blood

Ignatius of Loyola, the founder of the Jesuits, placed great emphasis on the theme of circumcision: according to him, it was the first time Jesus shed his blood. It thus forms the starting point for the first exercise in his famous book *Spiritual Exercises*.

As São Roque is a Jesuit church, it is not surprising that the painting of the circumcision occupies a prominent place in the cycle of seven paintings.

It should also be noted that, according to tradition, Jesus' foreskin, collected during the circumcision, is one of the very few existing relics of Jesus (along with his umbilical cord at birth and his milk teeth), who ascended to heaven body and soul at the Ascension.

In Rome, the church of San Filippo Neri also has two paintings on display in rotation. From the same publisher, see the guide *Secret Rome*.

THE SYMBOLS OF THE TOMB OF KING DOM FERNANDO I

A king in an alchemical tomb

Museum of Archeology – Largo do Carmo
Monday to Saturday, 10am–5pm
Metro Baixa-Chiado – Tram 24E

Damaged in the earthquake of 1755, which caused the building to collapse, the Gothic tomb of King Dom Fernando I (1345-1383) is now on display at the city's Museum of Archaeology. In addition to the coats of arms of Portugal and of the Manuel family (his mother was Dona Constança Manuel), the tomb is covered in hermetic symbols.

Dom Fernando I, who died on 23 October 1383 in Lisbon, ordered that he be dressed in a Franciscan habit and buried next to his mother at the São Francisco convent at Santarém. His remains were left here, however, in the former Carmel convent founded in 1389 by the Saint Constable Dom Nuno Álvares Pereira, which was later converted into a museum.

The king's affinities and closeness to the *Beguins** explains the presence of elements connected to them on this funerary monument that was nevertheless kept at the Carmelite site. On one side of the tomb, the scene of Saint Francis of Assisi's inspiration on Mount Alvernia is depicted. The saint is shown receiving the stigmata of the Lord, and next to him, there is a monastery and a staircase with a praying monk, a symbol of adoration, faith and obedience to the Franciscan order.

On the other side of the tomb, a curious seated figure attentively looks at a vase before him. A book lies at his feet and, behind him on either side, two shelves are lined with more vases. A symbol of an alchemical laboratory (*labor oratorium*), this illustration is related to the images below, two effigies of a monk and a lady (perhaps Dom Fernando's mother) who, in this context, symbolise the hermetic couple and the union of opposites that was indispensable to the realisation of the grand work of alchemy.

At the base of the tomb, two griffons with necks interlaced represent the alchemical *rebis*, another reminder of the necessary union of opposites for the realisation of the philosopher's stone, which itself is an allegory of the spiritual awakening that accompanies the fabrication of philosophical gold.

Contrary to King Dom Afonso V, nothing suggests that Dom Fernando I was an alchemist, even if he was undoubtedly close to several followers of this tradition.

*Beguins: *Franciscans (sometimes Dominicans) called the 'spiritual ones' who professed the purity of the origins of Christianity, combined with the hermetic concepts originating in alchemy, which they considered to be the representation of the 'path of perfection'.*

CERVEJARIA TRINDADE'S MASONIC AZULEJOS

Manuel Garcia Moreira, Master Mason, Third Degree

Rua Nova da Trindade, 20 C
Daily, 12pm to midnight
Metro Baixa-Chiado – Tram 24E

The refectory and part of the cloister of the former Lisbon Trinitarian convent are now the *Cervejaria Trindade* (Trinity Brasserie), one of the most distinguished restaurants in the city. On entering, you cannot fail to notice a series of polychrome azulejo panels along the wall clearly depicting Masonic themes.

Their creator, painter Luís Ferreira, the artistic director of the Viúva de Lamego factory, was better known as 'Ferreira das Tabuletas' (Shop Sign Ferreira) (1807-1870). He has left a rare example of his naive and popular style here. The saturated colours in strong chromatic contrasts are set in false recesses, like statue niches, thus imitating *trompe l'œil* painting.

It was the Galician Manuel Garcia Moreira who commissioned these panels from the artist after having bought the building of the former Trinity convent from Joaquim Peres in 1836. A converted Freemason, Garcia Moreira had azulejo panels made for his garden, the building's lateral facade, and the interior of the convent's former rectory. The lion's head symbol, repeated in profusion throughout the work, designates the third degree in the Masonic hierarchy, that of master mason.

The lion's claws, a symbol of the same rank that designates the resurrection of Hiram Abiff, the Phoenician architect of King Solomon's Temple, also occurs frequently.

In the above-mentioned false niches, there are other Masonic symbols, such as the allegorical representations of the luminous delta with the eye of the Supreme Architect inscribed in a radiant Sun. On another panel, the goddess Concordia, shown holding a rod and offering an olive branch to a dove, is the symbol of Concord (Universal Brotherhood). The column of force (*Bohaz*), featured on Solomon's Temple, was adopted into Masonic symbolism. It also appears, supported by a seated woman (passive); at her feet is a lion's head rising out of the clouds, symbolising Garcia Moreira himself.

THE SAINT CONSTABLE'S MAGIC SWORD

A sword inspired by King Arthur's Excalibur

Carmelite convent cloister
Largo do Carmo
Monday to Saturday, 10am–6pm
Metro Baixa-Chiado

A curious sword is exhibited in the ruined cloister of the *Convento do Carmo* (Carmelite convent). Although an identical sword can be found above the side door of the Nossa Senhora dos Remédios chapel in Sertã, it is said that the original is the one displayed at Lisbon's Military Museum, near Santa Apolónia.

Measuring three inches at its widest point, the sword is straight and sharp; its hilt is brass and is encircled by a brass spiral design. Engraved on one side of the blade is the inscription *Excelsus super omnes gentes Dominicus* (God the Highest above men). Engraved on the other side are the name *Maria*, the words *Dom Nuno Álvaro* within a circle, and a countermark depicting a cross interlaced with flowers. The piercings and engravings on the blade, beyond their decorative aspect, make the sword lighter and thus easier to manipulate. These engravings are reminiscent of runes (the letters of early Icelandic *Edda* literature). In practice, the enemy's blade could get caught in the grooves, meaning he could easily find himself disarmed.

This sword belonged to Saint Constable Dom Nuno Álvares Pereira (1360-1431). Since his youth, he had been strongly influenced by the myths of the Knights of the Round Table and their quest for the Holy Grail, or the Holy Chalice, a symbol of Inspiration by the grace of the Holy Spirit.

As an adult, he chose a military career and distinguished himself as a valiant defender of the kingdom. Searching for a magic sword like Excalibur, the sword of the mythic King Arthur, Pereira took his old sword to Fernão Vaz, the armourer of Santarém. Upon returning the refurbished sword, the armourer told him, in a prophetic tone, that he could pay him for the work when he became the Count of Ourém. Once he had, indeed, become count, Dom Nuno generously reimbursed this armourer who, in addition to being a blacksmith, was also an alchemist and prophet.

Thanks to his blessed Excalibur, pointed towards the heavens in order to invoke its power, Dom Nuno Álvares Pereira secured Portugal's independence, which was threatened by Castile. He then laid down his sword to symbolise the sign of the cross and joined the Order of Carmelites until the end of his days, living the exemplary life of a monk-knight.

The Carmelites: an order influenced by hermetism

The Carmelite Order, originally called the Order of the Brothers of the good adventurous Virgin Mary of Mount Carmel, was formed in 1206-1214 by a group of Latin laymen, probably former Crusaders, who were led by a man only known by the letter B (he was later identified as Brocardo). They lived in the region of Mount Carmel, a range of hills near Haifa, formerly known as Porfiria, in what is now Israel.

The word carmel means 'garden'. Many Christians lived on this hill as hermits according to the biblical tradition of the prophet Elijah who in the past had retreated into a cave to live in prayer and silence. Later, these penitent Christians received a rule of life from Saint Albert, Latin Patriarch of Jerusalem, who regrouped them into a typically hermetic order centred on Christ. The Carmelite rule was approved by Pope Honorius III in 1226, but the monks had to return to Western Europe, where they began spreading the *Hyperdulia*, the worship and veneration of Our Lady, thus becoming Europe's first Marian religious order.

At the beginning of the 14th century, the Carmelites arrived in Portugal and settled at Moura, in the Alentejo region. Saint Constable Nuno Álvares Pereira quickly befriended them due to his great devotion for the Virgin Mary. He even had the Carmelite Convent of Lisbon built to house the brotherhood. He himself entered the order at the end of his life as a penitent brother of the

Carmelites of the Ancient Observance, its oldest branch.

Later, in 1593, the Discalced Carmelite Order was founded, the result of reforms carried out by Saint Theresa of Avila and Saint John of the Cross.

The Carmelites also had a certain connection to the hermetic tradition, as certain historic events indicate.

They disapproved of Pope Clement V (the moral

assassin of the Order of the Templars) and supported the election of João XII, author of the *Bula Sabatina*. They also benefited from the protection of the Hospitaller Order of Saint John of Acre, the future Order of Malta. They were accused of confusing the Virgin Mary with Mary of Egypt, known for an alchemical process that bears her name – that of distilling water using fire, or the famous 'bain-marie'. Two enormous azulejo panels, once in the now-closed Piedade de Cascais convent, are now on display in the Castro Guimarães villa gardens. One of them incontestably proves the Carmelite Order's hermetic connection. It depicts the Triumphal Procession of the Virgin Mary in Glory seated on the Chariot, in front of which stand the archangels Michael and Gabriel (associated with the Sun and the Moon) and behind which is the procession of the 'Sons of Mary', that is to say the followers of alchemy, the science of the Holy Spirit – Saint Antoine, Saint Isabelle of Portugal, Saint Isabelle of Hungary, Saint Albert the Great, Raimundo Lúlio and Arnaldo de Vilanova, among others. The angels flying above, each of which show a distinctive sign of Carmelite hermetism, such as the coat of arms in the lower section, add a final touch to the work.

The strange story of the Braço de Prata (Silver Arm)

In Moscavide, right next to the Quinta do Cabeço, stands the *Quita do Candeeiro* (Chandelier), which was the convent the Discalced Carmelites came to after their flight from Estrela convent, which had been annexed to Lisbon's basilica, in 1834.

In their flight, the nuns took a curious 17th-century relic with them – the right arm of Saint Theresa of Avila kept in a silver reliquary.

The cult of the relic was so strong that its memory survived in a local place name. *Braço de Prata* station used to be the stop for Ribatejo pilgrims on their way to Olivais to worship the saint. Around 1930, the Carmelites of Candeeiro donated the holy reliquary to the family of Spanish general Franco who took it to Avila. Since then, its worship has died out, but its memory survives in the name *Braço de Prata*.

ROYAL DOOR
OF OUR LADY OF THE VICTORY
OF MOUNT CARMEL CONVENT

A completely forgotten door and staircase

Largo do Carmo – Carmo Convent side exterior
Metro Baixa-Chiado – Tram 24E

On leaving the famous Santa Justa lift to reach Largo do Carmo, hardly anyone notices the curious, boarded-up door to the right, in front of which is a beautiful staircase which used to lead to nowhere. It nevertheless holds significant historic meaning.

The Our Lady of the Victory of Mount Carmel convent was once sited opposite the hill where São Jorge castle stands, on the slopes of which stood the royal palace and Sé Cathedral. Between the two hills lay what is now the Rossio district, known as the *Valverde* (Green Valley) in the 14th and 15th centuries. Having abandoned military life for his religious vocation, Saint Constable Dom Nuno Álvares Pereira had this convent built in 1389. He was absolutely determined that the main building of Carmel convent should be built at this precise spot, in Lisbon, despite the technical difficulties of reinforcing the steep slopes and constructing the foundations of the church choir. When the foundations gave way twice, Dom Nuno vowed to rebuild them in bronze if they gave way yet again. On the third attempt, the most reputable architects of Lisbon were hired: Afonso, Gonçalo and Rodrigo Eanes. Several master masons were also hired (Lourenço Gonçalves, Estevão Vasques, Lourenço Afonso, and João Lourenço), as were workers to prepare and apply the lime, a specialised task that was entrusted to the Jews Judas Acarron and Benjamin Zagas. As each obstacle was overcome, another appeared, but the building was finally finished, becoming the most remarkable Gothic edifice of its time.

The royal palace and convent stood face to face and the route from one to the other passed through this *porta real* (royal door), now forgotten. Its fleur-de-lys decoration (see p. 38) is the royal symbol, officially adopted by Dom João I, the first member of the Avis dynasty, whose protector was the Saint Constable.

Note the inscriptions on the stones near the ground in front of the door. These images of fish, animals and birds survived the terrible earthquake of 1755, as did the staircase that led to Campo de Valverde and the royal palace.

THE FIVE-POINTED STAR OF GRANDELLA DEPARTMENT STORES

Grandella, a former Freemason entrepreneur

Edifício dos Antigos Armazéns Grandella (access via 2 streets)
Rua do Ouro, 205–217 – Rua do Carmo, 26–52
Monday to Saturday, 9am–1pm
Metro Baixa-Chiado

Carved on the columns between the Grandella department store doors, the Grandella motto, 'Always on the right path and moving forward', surrounds a five-pointed star. It is simply the Masonic star that Grandella adopted as his personal emblem. He had, in fact, been initiated to Freemasonry under the symbolic name of *Pilatos* and was affiliated to the José Estevão Lodge in Lisbon in 1910.

The *Amazéns Grandella* (Grandella Department Stores) have born the name of their owner, Francisco de Almeida Grandella (1852-1934), since 1891. A very wealthy businessman, Grandella arrived in Lisbon as a young man and grew rich thanks to his determination, honest work and sharp business sense. After acquiring his first building in 1890, Grandella bought the building on rua do Carmo, located just behind his establishment, in 1903, and had it demolished in order to create a new structure and enlarge his store. The majestic edifice was constructed by entrepreneur João Pedro dos Santos, after a design by French architect Georges Demay (who had designed the famous Printemps department stores in Paris). Engineer Ângelo de Sárrea Prado completed the project.

In April 1907, the building, described by its owner as '… a gigantic, audacious, refined accomplishment whose richness, elegance, good taste, reflection of light, crystal, gilded capitals, marble columns make you think of fairytales, of the Thousand and One Nights!' was finally

inaugurated. Lisbon now possessed the 'most beautiful and largest department stores in the entire Iberian Peninsula.'

The Grandella Department Stores, with their Art Nouveau style mixed with Portuguese decoration, thus opened to the public in 1907. After the great fire that destroyed the buildings in August 1980, the facade was restored. It was topped with a magnificent clock in which two blacksmiths sound the hours near the mythic figures of Truth and Commerce that had survived.

The symbolism of the pentragram, the five-pointed star

The pentagram is a five-pointed star composed of five straight lines. In Portuguese, pentagrama means a word with five letters. In music, it is also the five parallel lines that compose sheet music. Originally, it was the symbol of the Roman goddess Venus and, consequently, was associated with this planet as its orbit, as seen from Earth, apparently draws a five-pointed star every eight years, as illustrated by the astronomer Ptolemy.

In nature, the pentagram is the sign of the fifth element, Ether, which occupies the superior branch, while the other four elements (Air, Fire, Water, Earth) occupy the inferior branches.

The pentagram (or *pentalpha*) is also the symbol for Infinity. In the pentagon at the centre of the pentagram, another smaller pentagram can be drawn, and so on. It also possesses a numerical symbolism, always based on the number 5, which represents the marriage between the masculine (3) and the feminine (2), and thus symbolises the union of opposites that is necessary for spiritual realisation.

That is why, in the mathematics of the Pythagorean school of thought, the pentagram (the emblem of this Greek institution) is linked to the golden ratio (1.618). Composed of a regular pentagon and five isosceles triangles, the ratio between the side of the triangle and its base (the side of the pentagon) is equal to the golden number.

The Jewish Kabbalah, through its most learned rabbis, considers the pentagram to be the symbol of the will of God and of divine protection.

In Christianity, it is the star of Christmas and of Christ's birth, which predicts the Resurrection of both the spirit in the body (birth) and the body in the spirit (resurrection).

In Freemasonry, it is the Blazing Star of initiation. Placed in the eastern part of the Lodge, it also symbolises the resurrection, when the follower leaves the profane world to become a new initiate.

When the pentagram is shown upside-down, it generally becomes a symbol of Evil, the opposite of what it symbolises when upright (Good). It means that the Spirit has been plunged into the blindness of Matter and the physical suffering of the human soul.

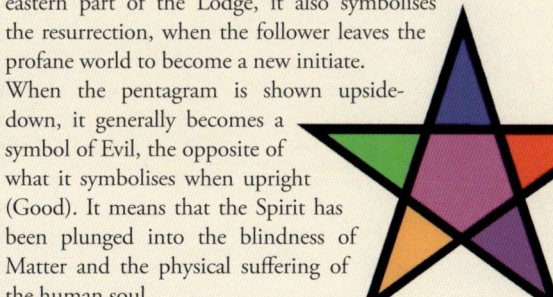

Lapa, Madragoa, Estrela, Campo de Ourique

EPIC OF THE HOLY CONSTABLE RELICS

He was a great prince, but he made himself a humble monk

Igreja de Santo Condestável – Campo de Ourique
Open during mass at 9am and 6pm
Tram 25E, 28E

In 1768, the bones of Dom Nuno that had survived the catastrophic 1755 earthquake were placed in a wooden copy of his coffin. They remained there until 1856 when they were removed and eventually placed in a velvet-lined urn in 1895. In 1912, the relics were placed in a silver reliquary and taken on a devotional pilgrimage around the country. Finally, they were stolen in 1967 and have never been recovered. Other bones, which had prudently been kept elsewhere, replaced the stolen ones. Some of these are venerated in the Terceira Order chapel at Largo do Carmo, while the rest are kept under the main altar at Santo Condestável church in Campo de Ourique.

The 1755 earthquake entirely destroyed the Carmo and Trindade neighbourhoods, which are still linked today in the famous saying *cair o Carmo e a Trindade* (knock down the Carmel and the Trinity). The Carmelite convent that Dom Nuno Álvares Pereira (1360-1431) had founded was razed to the ground and his tomb was lost. All that is left today are a few bones. Although his original tomb was a simple one, as he had requested, a more stately tomb was later constructed upon which was inscribed the following epitaph:

'Here lies that famous Nuno, the Constable, founder of the House of Bragança, excellent general, blessed monk, who during his life on earth so ardently desired the Kingdom of Heaven that after his death, he merited the eternal company of the Saints. His worldly honours were countless, but he turned his back on them. He was a great prince, but he made himself a humble monk. He founded, built and endowed this church in which his body rests.'

The tomb was located near the main altar and contained a single shroud-enveloped body. A sort of insulated drawer protected the head to keep it from touching the dirt and lime. This custom, which had fallen out of practice a century before Dom Nuno Álvares Pereira's death, was the same used by the legendary knights of the Round Table that had so inspired Dom Nuno since his childhood (see p. 144). Indeed, his mother, Dona Íria, had nicknamed him the little *Galaaz*, or Galahad, after the purest of the knights. People sometimes smashed the church floor in order to take a handful of holy earth from his miraculous grave. They considered him to be the last medieval knight, a model of justice and perfection.

Nuno Álvares Pereira, the miraculous 14th-century warrior canonsed in 2009

Also known as the Holy Constable, Nuno Álvares Pereira (born 26 June 1360 in Cernache de Bonjardim, Sertã; died 1 April 1431 at the convent of Carmo, Lisbon) was a noble Portuguese knight of the 14th century who played a fundamental role in the 1383-1385 crisis, when Portugal fought against Castile for its independence. He was also the 2nd Count of Arraiolos, the 7th Count of Barcelos, the 3rd Count of Ourém, and attained the rank of Constable in the Portuguese army, a position equivalent to what today would be the Minister of Defence. At his death, he had already acquired his saintly reputation. The son of Dom Álvaro Gonçalves Pereira, prior of the Order of Malta that was headquartered in the monastery at Flor da Rosa, in Crato, and of the noble-born Dona Íria Gonçalves do Carvalhal, Nuno Álvares Pereira grew up in his parent's home in Flor da Rosa. He learned the military arts and to enjoy reading, especially chivalrous stories in which 'purity was the virtue that made the heroes of the Round Table invincible', and where it was possible for 'one's soul and body to remain immaculate'. He dreamed, telling his mother that one day he would also be a Grail Knight, that he was going to find the Grail and place it on the altar of the Lusitanian homeland. From then on, his mother called him 'my little Galahad', after the hero who, according to the Round Table legend, succeeded in finding the Chalice. Galahad was also the nickname of Christ himself. At the age of 13, Pereira entered the court of Ferdinand I and was made a knight with armour loaned by Dom João, Master of the Order of Avis. On 15 August 1376, at the age of 16, he married Dona Leonor Alvim at Vila Nova da Rainha in Azambuja. They had a daughter, Beatriz, but Dona Leonor died soon after giving birth (1388). Years later, on 1 November 1401, Beatriz married Dom Afonso, the bastard son of Dom João I and the 1st Duke of Bragança, at Paço de Frielas in Loures. In 1383, when King Dom Fernando I died with princess Dona Beatriz (wife of King Dom João I of Castile) as his only heir, Dom Nuno Álvares was one of the first to support Dom João, Master of the Order of Avis, in his claim for the crown. Although he was the illegitimate son of Dom Pedro I of Portugal, crowning Dom João was preferable to losing the country's independence to the Castilians. After Dom Nuno Álvares' first military victory against the Castilians at the battle of Atoleiros in April 1384, Dom João of Avis named him Constable of Portugal and Count of Ourém. On 6 April 1385, the Master of the Order of Avis was proclaimed King of Portugal at Coimbra. It did not take long for the Castilians to retaliate, as their powerful army soon invaded the country. On 14 August of the same year, the Portuguese forces confronted the Castilians at Aljubarrota. Despite their large disadvantage in terms of numbers (one Portuguese warrior to ten Castilians), the Portuguese won their stunning victory in less than an hour, thanks to the military genius of the Constable, who thus became, from then on, the patron saint of the Portuguese army. The battle of Aljubarrota definitively marked the end of the country's political instability and reinforced its independence. On 25 July 1415, Dom Nuno Álvares Pereira set off with a fleet on expedition to Ceuta, in North Africa. It was his last battle. He later distributed his wealth to his family and the Carmelite Order (see p. 134) and became a mendicant monk at the Convent of the Carmelites in Lisbon. He had already earned his reputation as a saint, yet he kept his warrior soul. It is said that, when Ceuta ran the risk of being retaken by the Moors, the old, stooped warrior wanted to go to the rescue. When others tried to dissuade him, he grabbed a lance and threw it from the convent's balcony. The lance crossed the valley below and pierced a door on the other side of Rossio. Dom Nuno declared, 'If it were necessary, I could throw it all the way to Africa!' This is the source of the Portuguese expression 'to throw a lance to Africa', meaning to overcome a great difficulty. On 30 March 1431, a Good Friday, the 'Holy Brother,' as he was called, fell gravely ill. He died at noon on 1 April, Easter Sunday, at the age of 70. The Portuguese people mourned their Holy Warrior. When they visit the Holy Constable, as he is still known today, visitors take a handful of soil from his tomb. The Carmelite Chronicle says that this miraculous soil, mixed with water and swallowed, has produced 12 resurrections, healed 24 paralysed people, 21 blind people, 21 deaf and dumb people, 18 people suffering from internal diseases, 16 people suffering from fatal diseases, 10 people with fever and bleeding, and led to 6 apparitions of the Grand Knight in holy grace. The miracles attributed to Nuno Alvares led Pope Benedict XV to beatify him on 23 January 1918, attributing the feast day of 6 November to him. At 9:33am, on 26 April 2009, Pope Benedict XVI canonised him as Saint Nuno of Santa Maria.

TOMB OF THE COUNTESS OF EDLA

Copy of the Cruz Alta of Sintra

Cimitero dos Prazeres – Praça São João Bosco
Daily, 10am–5pm
Tram 25E, 28E

Elisa Hensler, Countess of Edla (1836–1929), was the second wife of King D. Fernando II. Like her husband, she had a great passion for the Serra de Sintra, to the extent that she wanted to erect a copy of the 'Cruz Alta' of Sintra over her tomb in the Prazeres Cemetery, even using stones brought from there.

When D. Fernando died, in 1885, he left his entire inheritance to his widow, including the Castelo dos Mouros and the Pena Palace, in Sintra. D. Carlos I was able to recover these properties by paying 410,000 escudos to the countess. After they were sold, Elisa Hensler abandoned Sintra and went to live with her daughter Alice in Lisbon, where she died at the age of 92 ... But not before she had added her last wishes regarding her tomb to her will of February 1928: 'A plot 4 metres in length shall be purchased. On it will be placed a copy of the cross located on the Cruz Alta in the Pena Park, in Sintra. The size of the cross must be appropriate for the plot. The following will be inscribed on the steps forming the base of the cross: 'Here lies Elisa Hensler, widow of His Majesty the King Fernando II, born 1836".

The Countess of Edla's grave was thus constructed in the Prazeres Cemetery, at number 6399 in Alley 2A, recreating the bucolic setting of the highest point of her beloved Serra de Sintra. The work of Raúl Lino, it consists of a stack of irregular-shaped granite blocks originating from the Serra and resting on a square limestone plinth, surrounded by dense vegetation. At its apex stands the copy of the Cruz Alta, the original of which is found at the highest point of the Pena Park.

This location is highly significant for some specialists in the esoteric, who have nicknamed it the 'Peak of the Grail', perhaps because it was there that King D. Fernando II recreated the paradisiacal setting of Richard Wagner's operas *Lohengrin* and *Parsifal*. The Countess of Edla owned a chalet, the first in the country, in a corner of the park, where she carried out experiments on plant species and painted motifs from Portuguese mythology on canvas or crockery. She was therefore no stranger to these esoteric references. After passing away in her Santa Maria Palace, located in the Coraçao de Jesus area of Lisbon, Elisa Friedericke Hensler, the Countess of Edla, singer, artist, painter, ceramist and nearly queen, enjoyed the treatment and honours due to a great figure of state. The deposed king and queen, D. Manuel II and Augusta Victoria, sent the Viscount of Asseca to represent them.

THE SYMBOLS OF CARVALHO MONTEIRO'S VAULT

The vault of the founder of Sintra's Quinta da Regaleira

Cimitero dos Prazeres
Praça São João Bosco
Daily, 10am–5pm
Tram 25E, 28E

Located at No. 1382 of alley 11 (on the left) of the Cemitério dos Prazeres (Cemetery of Pleasures), this family mausoleum was built for António Augusto de Carvalho Monteiro (Rio de Janeiro, 27 November 1848 – Sintra, 25 October 1920), whose coffin was laid to rest here on 2 April 1922.

A wealthy trader with degrees in law and philosophy, António Carvalho Monteiro was a highly cultured man, as is notably illustrated by his Quinta da Regaleira, the monumental palace he had built at Sintra between 1900 and 1910.

Here, on the vault, one finds the same post-Romantic and neo-Manueline tendencies as well as the mark of the Templar Seal that characterised his ideas of an Initiation to Portugality. He quenched his thirst for knowledge in the theosophical and hermetic writings of the prophet Bandarra, Dante's mythologies and especially the Portuguese prophecies and myths of Camões (see page 64).

Carvalho Monteiro turned to architect Luigi Manini to design this symbolically rich vault made from Carrara marble.

It is composed of three parts, the first of which shows the Archangel Michael, guardian of souls, who represents the heavens and the world above. On the door to the upper vault, a bee on an hourglass represents the passage of the human soul. The crypt, the underground lair of the immortals, is in the lower vault.

On either side of the vault facade stand traditional statues representing Faith holding a cross and Hope holding a chalice. Whereas Hope is bareheaded, the head of Faith is covered, thus illustrating that Faith is intimate, based solely on one's personal beliefs, while Hope is its supreme and ultimate affirmation.

THE DUKE OF PALMELA'S MASONIC VAULT

④

Europe's largest private funerary monument

Cimitero dos Prazeres – Praça São João Bosco
Daily, 10am to 5pm
Tram 25E, 28E

The Duque de Palmela family vault, built in 1849, stands out prominently in the Cemitério dos Prazeres (Cemetery of Pleasures), as it is the largest private funerary monument in Europe.

It has belonged to Lisbon Municipal Council since 1997, when it was donated by engineer Manuel de Sousa Holstein Beck, the 4th Count of Póvoa. Its imposing dimensions, clear Masonic influences, and exceptional works of art (such as Canova's cenotaph and the tomb of the Teixeira Lopes brothers) make a visit worthwhile.

This mausoleum, which holds the bodies of 200 members of the Palmela family and their household staff, is the reproduction of a temple in the form of an ancient Egyptian pyramid. Inside, several statues by well-known sculptors adorn the tombs.

Its construction was ordered by the 1st Duke of Palmela, Pedro de Sousa Holstein (Turin 1781 – Lisbon 1850), a Portuguese politician and military man with liberal ideas. Although he was not a member, he sympathised with the esoteric ideals of symbolic Freemasonry and entrusted the mausoleum project to architect José Cinatti, a well-known Freemason.

In Freemasonry, 7, 5 and 3 are considered perfect numbers. Thus 7 steps must be climbed to enter the vault, then 5 more to reach the crypt. The number 3, which represents the Trinity, is found in the front triangle of the pyramid, behind the mausoleum's Greek porch entrance. At its top is a sculpture of the Angel of Good Death holding a cross and a closed book, attributed to Calmels.

The vault layout was designed after Solomon's Temple, in which beginners and apprentices sat around the north pillar, also called the Feminine or Lunar (Bohaz) pillar, while the initiates and companions sat around the south pillar, or the Masculine or Solar (Jakin) pillar. Here, the female servants are buried on the left (the north side), and the male servants on the right (the south side). Inside the chapel, on the east side, lies the Palmela family, thus representing the master initiates. Solomon's Temple is believed to have been paved with black and white stones, and here, too, the entrance to the mausoleum is laid with square stones of the same colour.

FONTE SANTA
DOS PRAZERES

The miraculous waters of a legendary fountain

Rua Coronel Ribeiro Viana
Tram 28E

At the turn in rua Coronel Ribeiro Viana in the Cemitério dos Prazeres (Cemetery of Pleasures), between numbers 11-D and 13, you will find the Fonte Santa dos Prazeres (Holy Fountain of Pleasures), almost hidden between modern buildings that have completely transformed the local landscape.

This fountain, after which this location is named, consists of a smooth, ochre-coloured back panel that has a lintel of white marble stretching across the entire width of the base. The basin that lies under the lintel is still the original, but has been restored several times. Inside, you can see a stone block where jars were placed and that still shows the marks of the iron supports. On the backplate, which ends in a cross, is a carved stone dating from the 16th century representing a boat whose prow forms a snake's head. It was placed there in 1835 during restoration work.

The water flowing from the fountain, from a spring-loaded metal tap, no longer comes from the spring that once fed it and that was said to heal the sick. The spring, which supposedly dried up due to the construction of the neighbouring buildings, was replaced by water from the EPAL network (Lisbon Water Supply company).

According to legend, a statue of the *Senhora dos Prazeres* (Our Lady of Pleasures) appeared over the spring, thus bestowing its water with virtuous healing powers. The Lisbon Senate consequently decided to have the tank and basin built, and to affix a gargoyle with the town's coat of arms there. The statue was later placed in a chapel built for it, but which no longer exists.

The chapel was sited on land named after its patron, the Quinta dos Prazeres, which is now used as the cemetery. Many people attended the chapel's Sunday services, especially those on the Sunday and Monday after Easter week because all of the religious brotherhoods, priests and monks of the Santos parish walked in procession, with crosses raised, singing a solemn mass. The chapel would have stood just above the Fonte Santa, in what is now rua Coronel Ribeiro Viana, before Travessa dos Prazeres, at No. 27.

The Fonte Santa's snake ship and the name 'Our Lady of Pleasures' evoke the concept of happiness in the afterlife through a holy water ritual healing both body and soul.

THE INTERIOR GARDEN
OF THE SÃO BENTO PALACE

One of the city's hidden treasures

Palace of the Assembly of the Republic
Praça de São Bento
Assembly of the Republic Information Centre
213 919 625
Visits last Saturday of every month (3pm and 4pm)
Free guided tours
Tram 8E

The former monastery of São Bento da Saúde, now the palace of the Assembly of the Republic, is home to a magnificent garden, an oasis of delight and tranquillity, which may be visited on the last Saturday of the month.

Situated behind the palace, this interior garden designed by the architect Luís Cristino da Silva (1896–1976) is characterised by French-inspired symmetry in the layout of its flower beds and statues. It is divided into four terraced levels, a perfect solution to the difficulties presented by the steeply sloping terrain. The garden is separated from the Prime Minister's official residence by a 50 metre-long wall, punctuated by sixteen recesses and the same number of fountains, along with a double stairway (also by Cristino da Silva), constructed in the 1940s and leading to the upper garden. It is crowned with two sphinxes bearing the emblem of the Portuguese flag, the work of António Leopoldo de Almeida. Standing on either side of the steps, a short distance to the front, there are two beautiful statues symbolising power and justice. This beautiful, little-known garden deserves an in-depth tour. Its construction, in the mid-20th century, evokes the original green area located behind the wall of the Benedictine Monastery of São Bento da Saúde, founded by the Archabbot D. Frei Baltasar de Braga in 1598. After the dissolution of the religious orders in Portugal, in 1834, the building became the Palácio das Cortes, on the orders of D. Pedro IV.

Since the *Estado Novo* (the Salazar dictatorship), that is to say after 1975–76, it has housed the Assembly of the Republic. Throughout these years, it was clear that the gardens (which were destroyed in the 1755 earthquake) needed restoration. This task was undertaken by Cristino da Silva, thanks to whom one of the city's most beautiful hidden treasures has been brought back to life.

GERMAN CEMETERY
IN LISBON

A final rural retreat

Rua do Patrocínio, 59
213 900 439
Tuesday to Sunday, 9am–1pm
Closed December 24, 25 and 31, and January 1
Guided tours by reservation
Tram 25E, 28E

Few Lisbon residents have ever heard of their city's German Cemetery. Located between the iconic Cemitério dos Prazeres (Cemetery of Pleasures) and the Basilica da Estrela, concealed from prying eyes behind high walls, the only indication is a small blue-and-white azulejo panel bearing the inscription *Cemitério Alemão – Deutsche Evangelische Kirchengemeinde* (German Cemetery – German Protestant Church).

To visit, ring the bell at the heavy green door leading to the lovely gardens.

The history of the cemetery goes back to 1821, when wealthy merchant Nicolaus Berend Schlick from Lübeck donated to the German evangelical community a plot of land of around 3,000 m² in the heart of what is now Campo de Ourique district.

Without his generosity, the Germans of Lisbon might still be buried in the nearby British Cemetery (see p. 158), which previously accepted bodies from the German Protestant community. Schlick's portrait can be seen in the small chapel.

Since it was opened on 25 January 1822, this burial ground has offered eternal rest to all Germans living in Portugal, whether Protestant, Catholic or Jewish, as well as anyone married to a German resident.

A secular German presence

Lisbon has been home to a large German community for centuries. The first arrivals, Crusaders who had taken part in the reconquest of Portuguese territory occupied by the Moors, date back to 1147. The German cavalrymen who died in battle are buried under the sacristy of São Vicente de Fora convent, dedicated to Saint Vincent to commemorate the victory of the Crusaders against the Muslim armies.

BRITISH CEMETERY

A piece of England in the heart of Lisbon

Rua de São Jorge, 15 – Estrela – Tram 25E, 28E
Daily, 10am to 5pm

Although it is open to the public every day, the British Cemetery is one of Lisbon's best-kept secrets. Small and hidden, sheltered by high walls and shaded by hundred-year-old towering trees, this is one of the most romantic, and yet little-known, green spaces in the city. It is a perfect complement to the Estrela Garden whose north entrance is located directly opposite, on the other side of the street, and which post-dates the cemetery (1842). The site was granted to the British and Dutch communities in 1717 for the purpose of creating a cemetery on the neighbouring plot at la Travessa dos Ladrões, the present-day Rua da Estrela. At that time, Protestants were persecuted by Catholics, who considered them to be heretics, despite the de facto freedom of worship that had existed in Portugal since the Restoration of 1640.

Also known as the Cemetery of the Cypresses, a nickname derived from the Inquisition court's need to plant a wall of cypresses around its perimeter in order to prevent Catholics from seeing Protestant graves, this site was described at the time as 'heretic ground'.

Thus, as well as being one of the most beautiful cemeteries in Lisbon, this site is also an excellent repository for the long and turbulent history of the British presence in Portugal. The oldest gravestone, which has been

worn down over the years, is situated close to the entrance. The remains of Francis La Roche, a Huguenot refugee, have lain here since 1742. The date is surprising given that the Luso-Britannic alliance was formed much earlier (1373). However, from the 16th century, as a result of the famous schism initiated by Henry VIII, most of the English population ceased to obey the Pope. This meant that Anglicans living in Catholic countries faced numerous difficulties, including the ban on being buried in the existing cemeteries. In Portugal, Protestants – whether residents or just passing through – were therefore buried in secret, next to the sea or by rivers.

The most famous gravestone in the cemetery, and the only one to be signposted from the entrance through the wall, is that of Henry Fielding, 'the father of the English novel' and the author of *Tom Jones*, published in 1749. Fielding left for Portugal in an attempt to restore his health but died on arrival in 1754, leaving behind the posthumous work he drafted aboard ship, *Journal of a Voyage to Lisbon*.

Many of the oldest and most 'artistic' tombs and mausoleums in the cemetery date from the second half of the 18th century. They include a number of Englishmen identified as retired soldiers in Lisbon at the time of their withdrawal, but who had never served in Portugal. The same cannot be said of the following generation and those who died on the battlefields of the Napoleonic Wars (1799–1815) in such great numbers that it became necessary to enlarge the enclosure, which was then known as the Soldiers' Cemetery.

St. George's (São Jorge) Church, which is now closed, was founded on this plot in 1822. Almost all of the graves are topped with shrubs, the oldest alleys are covered in moss, while enormous dragon trees, towering cypresses and giant palms stand among the Gothic tombs and Celtic crosses.

THE MOUSE OF RATO SQUARE

Homage to a 17th-century canon

Largo do Rato, 10B
Metro Rato

In front of number 10B Largo do Rato, an anthracite mouse has been worked into the *calçada portuguesa* (Portuguese pavement) (see box). This example of *empedrados* is a reference to the origins of the square, which is associated with the second canon of the monastery of Our Lady of Remedies of the Sisters of the Order of the Holy Trinity, also known as the monastery of Rato (Monastery of the Mouse).

Recently converted to Christianity and ennobled, Manuel Gomes de Elvas founded this monastery in 1621. It was his successor, Luís Gomes de Sá e Menezes, who completed its construction between 1675 and 1721. Gringalet, dressed in grey and scurrying about with small, rapid steps, with his elongated nose, soon acquired the nickname '*rato*' (mouse). A celebrated figure in the neighbourhood, he gave his name to the priory and then the crossroads, which has retained this name for four centuries, despite a failed attempt to rename it Brazil Square between 1910 and 1948.

Now occupied by a social security office and a municipal police station, the priory no longer accommodates nuns but its church continues to welcome the faithful. To its left, the magnificent pink palace constructed in 1784 on the site of the former Royal Porcelain Factory was last owned by the Marquis da Praia e Monforte. Since 1986, it has housed the Socialist Party headquarters.

Between Rua da Escola Politécnica and Rua do Salitre, the baroque Rato fountain (1744), made of Lioz stone, was the first in the city to be incorporated into the Águas Livres Aqueduct project. Managed by three water companies, its three taps supplied the district and employed about 100 delivery men. This ingenious network led to the Royal Porcelain and Silk Factory being established in the vicinity.

Calceteiro, a dying craft

Battered, broken and smooth, *calçada portuguesa* (Portuguese pavement) has since 1849 decorated the pavements, squares and streets of the capital and its former colonies (Brazil, Mozambique, Madeira). The blocks of grey basalt and white limestone that create pictures are called *empedrados* (literally, 'paved'). This type of paving owes its existence to Eusébio Pinheiro Furtado, lieutenant general and commander of the army, who drew inspiration from the Roman technique in order to keep the prisoners of São Jorge Castle occupied. The city of Lisbon was so pleased with the effect that it ordered more. There are now only twenty *calceteiros* (the workers who create and meticulously maintain these mosaic pavements) remaining in Lisbon. The city authorities opened a master pavers' school in 1986. However, it is struggling to recruit young apprentices, who do not enjoy working crouched down for such low wages. In 2006, a bronze statue of a calceteiro was erected on Rua da Vitória in honour of this dying craft.

UNDERGROUND VISIT
TO THE LORETO GALLERY

A fascinating underground tour to the source of Lisbon's water supply

Mãe d'Água das Amoreiras
Praça das Amoreiras 10 (or sometimes to the Aqueduct of the Príncipe Real)
Visits possible a couple of times a month, on Saturdays
Reservations: 218 100 215 or mda.epal@adp.pt
Closed-toe shoes recommended
Children under the age of 6 are not allowed
Tram 24E

A couple of times a month, on Saturdays and by reservation only, it is possible to walk through part of the underground galleries of the Aqueduct das Águas Livres (free waters), located between the Patriarchate reservoir, under the Príncipe Real garden, and the Mãe d'Água das Amoreiras reservoir, in the company of an authorised guide. The visit lasts approximately one and a half hours (including a 30 to 40-minute walk) and allows you to explore the two reservoirs.

The Amoreiras one is certainly the most interesting, as it is still filled with water and sometimes concerts, exhibitions and shows are organised there.

It may seem strange that the city of Lisbon, located on the banks of a river, does not have accessible drinking water sources for its entire population. In reality, due to its proximity to the Atlantic Ocean, the Tagus has a high salinity level that makes its water too salty for human consumption up to 40 kilometres inland. Moreover, for a long time, rainfall has been low in Lisbon: until a few centuries ago, it rained on average only four to five days a year. Today, however, the situation has improved and it currently rains about 45 to 50 days a year. The subsoil of the western part of the city, on the other hand, is largely made up of limestone, which does not allow for the retention of water and, consequently, the formation of natural underground water reservoirs; this is why it was necessary to build aqueducts outside the city perimeter.

Along the underground walk, the guides will also expertly tell you the exciting history of Lisbon's water supply, which began with the westward expansion of the capital from the 16th century onwards. During a period of political and financial stability, D. Joao V saw the need to modernise the city and put an end to the region's lack of access to drinking water. He thus decided to build the Aqueduct das Águas Livres (1731–1799) that would bring water from the Belas area within a radius of 58 kilometres. In the 19th century, as the population and, consequently, the need for water increased, the capacity of the aqueduct was greatly improved by the construction of new underground aqueducts: Francesas, Brouco and Matta.

On the first Sunday of the month, there is free access to the Mãe d'Água das Amoreiras reservoir (10am–1pm) and the Aqueduct das Águas Livres (10am–5.30 pm).

THE WINDOWS OF THE AUTOPALACE

An Art Nouveau jewel

Rua Alexandre Herculano, 66 – Metro Rato
937 780 434
Daily, 8am–9pm

N ot far from Largo do Rato, the red neon sign in front of the Continente Bom Dia supermarket sometimes draws the eye of passers-by to this building, which once housed a garage called Auto Palace. Indeed, it is easy to notice its magnificent stained glass window, crowned with Art Nouveau ceramics, on the gable of the building on which the name 'Auto Palace' stands out against a blue background. Built starting in 1906 by the Portuguese Automobile Company, the building has been listed, and although it no longer houses a garage, you can still enter the supermarket to admire a little secret: to the left of the main hall, which occupies 2,200 square metres, a remarkable stained glass window by C. Martins decorates what used to be the garage's offices, obviously car-themed. The work of C. Martins, these two superb stained-glass windows date back to 1907 and it is almost impossible to see them from the street, due to the poor lighting. Built by French architects Vieillard and Touzet (the creators of Central Tejo, the city's former power station now converted into a contemporary art gallery as well as a museum of electricity and the Napolitana factory), the Auto Palace is one of Lisbon's rare glass and steel buildings.

NEARBY
The building at 57 Alexandre Herculano Street
Right in front of the Auto Palace is the home of Miguel Ventura Terra, a Portuguese architect from the turn of the century who trained in France alongside Victor Laloux (the architect of the Gare d'Orsay) and won the Valmor Prize for architecture on several occasions. Ventura Terra also designed the synagogue in Lisbon, near his home.

NATIVITY SCENE
IN THE BASILICA DA ESTRELA

One of the largest nativity scenes in the world

Praça da Estrela
Basilica: 8.45am–8pm
Nativity scene: daily, 10am–11.30am and 3pm–5pm; closed on Sunday
Terrace: 9.30am–11.45am and 2pm–6.45pm; closed on Sunday morning
Tram 25E, 28E

In the right aisle of the transept of Estrela basilica, behind the tomb of Queen Mary I of Portugal (who had the church built to keep her promise to God after she gave birth to a son and heir), a little room contains one of the largest nativity scenes in the world.

In 1781 the Queen commissioned master sculptor Joaquim Machado de Castro to create a nativity scene for the Carmelite nuns in the convent next to the basilica. He was also responsible for the equestrian statue of Dom José I, the queen's father, that stands in Praça do Comercio.

Machado de Castro's Christmas crib has over 500 statuettes. The precision of the figures' clothing, their tools and the various background elements – some carved from Alentejo cork – is extraordinary. In the upper part are scenes of the Massacre of the Innocents and the Flight into Egypt. Right in the centre is the nativity scene, framed by Corinthian columns and surmounted by Baroque angels floating on clouds.

Lisbon's Museu Nacional de Arte Antiga (National Museum of Ancient Art) has a permanent exhibition of nativity scenes.

The roof of the basilica has a unique view of the Tagus and São Jorge castle, not to mention the modern tower blocks of Amoreiras district.

Nativity scenes, a venerable national tradition, usually spend eleven months of the year in 'maquinetas', small cupboards or showcases specially made for them. Unlike the permanent crib in the basilica, they are usually only on show to the public one month before Christmas.

FACADE OF CASA DO VISCONDE DE SACAVÉM

An assault on good taste?

Rua do Sacramento à Lapa, 24
Tram 28E

In the upper reaches of Estrela district, the facade of the Viscount of Sacavém's residence stands out clearly from its neighbours because of its numerous multicoloured ceramics.

The mixture of techniques and forms, busts, naturalistic shapes, carved ropes and enamelled spheres at the corners of the building are a tribute to the art of ceramics, although some people see it as 'an assault on good taste'.

The building, designed by architect Henrique Faria Blanc between 1897 and 1900, was embellished by the owner, a ceramicist at the school in the nearby spa town of Caldas da Rainha.

A pupil of Bordalo Pinheiro and Bernardo de Palissy, he was also the founder of the Campolide ceramics factory, known for its enamelwork.

The Viscount of Sacavém was also a collector and the patron of a number of ceramicists from Caldas da Rainha ('caldenses'). His romantic hunting lodge in that district was converted into a ceramics museum in 1983.

SECRETS OF NUNO GONÇALVES' POLYPTYCH

A coded message?

Museu Nacional de Arte Antiga – Rua das Janelas Verdes
Tuesday to Sunday, 10am–6pm
Closed Monday
Tram 15E, 18E

On show at the Museu Nacional de Arte Antiga (National Museum of Ancient Art), Nuno Gonçalves' polyptych (comprising two large panels and four narrower ones) is a masterpiece of Portuguese painting from the end of the Middle Ages and beginning of the Renaissance. Its creator, Nuno Gonçalves, royal artist for Dom Afonso V from 1450 onwards, is believed to have died in 1492.

It is said that this polyptych, of a rather sober yet strongly realistic style, was painted at the Paço Real (Royal Palace) of Sintra. It was not discovered until 1882, when Rafael Bordalo Pinheiro and his sister realised that workers were using it as scaffolding during restoration work on the patriarchate of São Vicente de Fora. They saved it from destruction without delay and began to restore it. However, it was not until 1931, when the work was exhibited in Paris, that Nuno Gonçalves

How the figures in the polyptych are arranged:

17 =	3	3	11	11	4	2	= 17
13 =	3	4	6	6	4	3	= 13

		=			=	
	13		17	17		13

won the international recognition he deserved. In a superb yet enigmatic manner, the polyptych illustrates the entire Lusitanian epic of the Avis dynasty. The 60 figures portrayed in the work have given rise to endless debates regarding their identification and placement, as well as the correct order of the panels.

The first panel is that of the Monks, shown dressed in the attire of the Cistercian Order, and the second, that of the Navigators, which shows crown prince Henrique kneeling at the front. In the centre of the third panel, that of the Pontiff, is a saint that resembles the Coptic and Byzantine representations of Prester John (Melkitzedek), King of Salem (representing heaven on earth) and priest of God Most High (representing the celestial paradise), and not, as some biblical scholars have claimed, Saint Vincent, Saint Catherine, the crown prince Dom Ferdinand, or the cardinal of Lisbon, James of Portugal. As in the scriptures, the saint is shown with the Gospel of Saint John open at the Pentecostal mass (see following double page). The same saint is found on the Monarch panel (the fourth), holding the King of the World's sceptre; the ropes at his feet outline a map of Portugal. The fifth panel is that of the Knights, and the sixth that of the Relic, showing a bone from the skull of Saint Anthony of Lisbon and Padua. Sixty figures are portrayed in all: 6 in the first panel, 7 in the second, 34 in the third and fourth, 8 in the fifth and 5 in the sixth. According to ancient Kabbalistic numerology, the number 60 represents Evolution. By dividing it by the double 3, and ignoring the zero that represents the abstract or nothingness, one obtains the Holy Trinity on earth and in the heavens and towards which all living things strive.

Two other important numbers are 13 (illustrated in the number of figures portrayed in the first two and last two panels) and 17 (the number of characters in each of the central panels). The number 13 symbolises the Immortality of the human soul after death. It is also the number that is traditionally attributed to Saint Mary and the Holy Spirit, to whom Portugal is dedicated.

The number 17 symbolises the hope for Immortality that the Word of God (as revealed in the open copy of the Gospel of Saint John) transmits to the congregation or, in other words, all of humanity. The number 17 also has a special meaning for Portugal. It is its own esoteric arcanum and designates the country as the ultimate hope for a new global spiritual empire (see p. 123).

> In addition to a sword and a pair of scales, the iconic symbols of Melkitzedek, King of the World (see p. 172), include the episcopal cross and book, which represent the Temporal and Spiritual powers. The polyptych's saint bears exactly these symbols.

Melki-Tzedek and Prester John: myth and reality

According to Judaeo-Christian tradition, the name Melkitzedek, earlier known as Melki-Tzedek, refers to the role of 'King of the World'. In charge of the Earth's evolution, he is the closest to God, and his function joins with that of God. In the Bible, the first reference to Melki-Tzedek appears in Genesis 14:18-20. 'And Melchizedek king of Salem brought forth bread and wine: and he was the priest of the most high God. And he blessed him, and said, Blessed be Abram of the most high God ... And he gave him tithes of all.' This thus established the Order mentioned in Psalms 110:4: 'Thou art a priest for ever after the order of Melchizedek.' In Hebrews 7:1-3, Saint Paul describes it as follows: 'For this Melchizedek, king of Salem, priest of the most high God, who met Abraham ... and blessed him; To whom also Abraham gave a tenth part of all; first being by interpretation King of righteousness, and after that also King of Salem, which is, King of peace; Without father, without mother, without descent, having neither beginning of days, nor end of life; but made like unto the Son of God; abideth a priest continually.' This is why the Christian Church identified him with the Third Person of the Trinity, the Holy Spirit, and with the guardian of the apostolic tradition that began with Peter the Apostle, so much so, in fact, that the Sacrifice of Melki-Tzedek (bread and wine) is generally seen as a 'foreshadowing' of the Eucharist. Theoretically, Christian priests identify with the priesthood of Melki-Tzedek, as Psalm 110 also applies to Christ. By referring to this mysterious king, the books of Genesis and Hebrews led the Judaeo-Christian tradition to distinguish between two priesthoods: one 'according to the Order of Aaron', and the other 'according to the Order of Melki-Tzedek'. The latter is superior to the former as it connects the present to the time of the coming of the Messiah and is related to the apostles, bishops and the Western Church. Aaron, on the other hand, connects the past to the present through the prophets, patriarchs and the Eastern Church. Melki-Tzedek is thus both king and priest. His name means 'king of Righteousness' and king of Salem, or 'king of Peace', 'Righteousness' and 'Peace' being exactly the two fundamental attributes of the 'King of the World'. The word Salem designates the 'City of Peace,' the archetype according to which Jerusalem was built, and which became the secret residence of the 'King of the World'. In the trans-Himalayan tradition, this city is called *Agharta* or *Shambala* and corresponds to the Terrestrial Paradise or the Primordial Eden that the Lusitanian myth insistently identifies with the future Fifth Empire of the World (see p. 64) which will mark the coming of the Kingdom of Happiness, ruled by Melki-Tzedek, the Universal Emperor. The equivalent of Melki-Tzedek in Ancient Egypt was Ptah; in India, he is called *Chakravarti*. The Rosicrucians knew him as *Rotan*, which is why the Freemasons recognised him under the name of *Incognito Superior*, or the *Universal Emperor*, in the 18th century. In the 12th century, in France, under the reign of Saint Louis, Carpin and Rubruquis in their travel accounts replaced the name of Melki-Tzedek with that of *Preste João* (Father or Prester John), who supposedly lived in a mysterious country at the northern edge of Asia. *Preste* means 'Father' and 'Priest' while John is a reference both to John the Baptist and John the evangelist who wrote the Apocalypse, a clear reference to the King of the World priesthood. The three religions of the Book (Judaism, Christianity and Islam) equally declare that it is through him that the Kingdom of Universal Harmony will come to Earth. Word of Prester John first arrived in Europe in 1145, when Hugo de Gebel, a bishop of the Christian colony in what is now Lebanon, told the pope of the existence of a Christian kingdom located 'beyond Persia and Armenia' that was ruled by a king-priest called *Johannes Presbyter* (John the Priest). He was supposedly the descendent of one of the Three Kings that went to see the Baby Jesus in Bethlehem. The first known document from this mysterious individual is the famous *Letter of Prester John*, sent to Manuel I Comnenus, Byzantine emperor of Constantinople, as well as to Frederick I Barbarossa, emperor of Germany, and to Pope Alexander III. The document apparently came from Portugal. The oldest version of the original text can be found in the Alcobaça monastery library and dates from the end of the 14th century. Published for the first time in Italian, at Venice in 1478, the letter inspired other Italian works, such as the rhymed version *Tratacto del maximo Prete Janni* (Venice?, 1494) by Giuliano Dati. In roughly the same period, Marco Polo, who had just returned to Venice, mentioned the existence of a Priest John, whom he believed to be the sovereign of the Ethiopian Church. Throughout the 15th and 16th centuries, another series of letters from Prester John appeared, this time sent from India to Portuguese rulers (João II, Manuel I and even Sebastião I, who is also said to have welcomed an ambassador sent by Prester John in his palace in Lisbon). The Portuguese kings also sent ambassadors to Prester John's court, as was notably the case for Pêro da Covilhã, sent by Dom Afonso V. The myth of Prester John was widely spread by the Knights Templar and constituted a strong impetus for Portugal's maritime discoveries.

SYMBOLISM OF THE TWO-HEADED MANUELINE FOUNTAIN

The alchemical hermaphrodite fountain

Museu Nacional de Arte Antiga – Tram15E, 18E
Tuesday to Sunday, 10am–6pm
Closed Monday

The strangest piece on display in the Museu Nacional de Arte Antiga is, without a doubt, the *fonte bicéfala* (two-headed fountain), which the museum bought from a private owner in 1939.

Created in a 16th-century Lisbon workshop between 1501 and 1515, this limestone fountain was destined to supply the town with water. It is now the rarest municipal artefact in the museum's Portuguese sculpture collection. With a twisted column characteristic of Manueline style, this fountain brings together two crowned heads and two embossed coats of arms showing an armillary sphere and a fisherman's net, the respective symbols of Dom Manuel I and Dona Leonor, his third wife.

This work, whose origin and characteristic anthropomorphic representation continue to mystify art historians, holds significant symbolic meaning. The snake-like scales decorating the twisted column are a clear allusion to water, an element guarded by this reptile and which was controlled by the king, who ensured its fair distribution.

In Portugal, the 16th century was a period of contrasts – modernism and conservatism, innovation and tradition – characterised in Manueline art. Although, on the one hand, works from this period illustrate the persistence of medieval models, on the other they portray Franco-Italian innovations that, in sculpture, arrived in Portugal either through the direct importation of works or through the Iberian and French master-builders who sojourned in the country.

In this work, the union of the fisherman's net and the armillary sphere is very rare (the only other example can be seen at Pelourinho de Óbidos). It is an unequivocal symbol of the marriage between Dona Leonor of Austria and Dom Manuel I of Portugal.

As for the serpent, it is an ancient symbol of the earth, due to its slithering nature, but also of the primitive waters of the Ocean. It thus also represents the source of life for all the creatures of the Earth.

Dom Manuel I was a staunch supporter of hermetic philosophy, which was very fashionable at the time. So this work probably also symbolises the Rebis (or Alchemical Hermaphrodite), which represents the union of opposites that is necessary for man's spiritual fulfilment.

Belém, Santo Amaro, Ajuda

SÃO JERÓNIMO CHAPEL

The forgotten chapel of Boitaca

Avenida Torre de Belém
213 620 034
Open for visits on Wednesdays by reservation at the educational offices of
Jerónimos monastery

The chapel of São Jerónimo (Saint Jerome) is located in a beautiful garden at the upper end of the grounds of Santa Maria de Belém monastery, a site that provides one of the finest panoramic views of the river and part of the city. Designed by Frenchman Diogo de Boytac (Boitaca), the architect of the Jerónimos monastery's first phase, the chapel's construction was begun in 1514 and was completed in 1517 through the work of the Portuguese master Rodrigo Afonso. The chapel's design is a square with sides measuring roughly 11 metres. Six Renaissance-style gargoyles stand out on the smooth walls, and a small cross presides over the main facade. The upper part of the front door, which is very small, is decorated with Manueline armorial symbols – five coats of arms, a crown and armillary spheres.

A triumphal arch with multiple lobes and spikes on its pendentives and cable moulding stands inside the chapel. Above the keystone can be seen the coat of arms of Saint Jerome. The nave's vault is a fine architectural model, illustrating elegant craftsmanship and rich in decorations that are identical to those of the starred dome. Although the apse once had three altars covered in 15th-century Sevillian azulejos, the current structure dates from the 20th century, but still displays the original panels.

This chapel, where Pina Manique (1733-1805), the founder of the Casa Pia of Lisbon, was buried, is one of the three chapels that King Dom Manuel I had built in Belém at each end of the vast Jerónimos monastery grounds. The other two chapels are Ermida de Nossa Senhora do Restelo (Our Lady of Restelo), which was built during the time of crown prince Dom Henrique but has not survived to the present day, and Santo Cristo, near the 'Os Belenenses' football stadium. In a sense, these three chapels symbolised the Trinity: the chapel of Christ represented the Father; the chapel of Our Lady of Restelo, the Mother; and that of Saint Jerome, the Son.

Manueline Art: of transition from darkness to light, often present in door and window ornamentation

Manueline art, sometimes also called Portuguese Late or Flamboyant Gothic, is a style of architecture, sculpture and furniture developed in the 16th century during the reign of Dom Manuel I. It is a Portuguese variation of Late Gothic and Lusitanian-Moorish or Mudejar art, characterised by the systematic use of its own iconographic motifs, generally large in size to symbolise royal power. The term 'Manueline' was coined by Francisco Adolfo Varnhagen in his work *Notícia Histórica e Descritiva do Mosteiro de Belém* (History and Description of the Monastery of Belém) in 1842.

At the time, this Manueline artistic trend was known as a Portuguese variation of *ad modum hispaniae* (Spanish-style) architecture, which itself was part of the *ao moderno* (modern) movement (later to be known as Late Gothic). This architectural movement contrasted with ancient style or Roman architecture.

It was Frenchman Jean Boytac, leader of the Master Builders brotherhood, who officially introduced the Manueline style to Portugal, with his first attempts on the royal palace of Sintra and his masterpiece, the monumental Jerónimos (Hieronymite) monastery of Belém. Manueline style is above all a style of passage, of transition from darkness to light, which explains why it is predominantly found in the ornamentation of doors and windows.

However, it does not hide the structure of the building, as superfluous ornamentation is avoided; the exterior and interior walls are generally left bare. Structural elements in areas of passage, such as columns, pillars, arches, friezes, oeils-de-boeuf and buttresses, as well as other elements such as tombs, fountains and religious monuments, are extensively decorated.

Manueline style, which is essentially a decorative art, is also characterised by the application of specific technical formulas regarding height, such as the multi-ribbed columns and vaults. It is precisely in sculpture that Manueline style reveals its greatest maturity and hegemony, because its decorative symbolism is recognised as a purely Portuguese style, and not as a variation of the style of other European countries. In this context, the sculptors and architects of Portugal inscribed a style of dynamic originality into the Portuguese artistic heritage, a style that astonishes still today.

The artistic 'discourse' present in Manueline style was considerably influenced by the personality of King Dom Manuel I (1469-1521) as well as by his desire to organise a crusade that would unify the Western

Christian world and Prester John's mythic Christian kingdom of the East (see p. 172). He would thus become the 'King of the Seas' (a name some foreign authors in fact called him).

Manueline style principally transmits these messianic aspirations of a king whose accession to power was unusual, to say the least. He became king after the successive deaths of the other direct heirs to the throne (such as prince Dom Afonso and his brother Dom Diogo, who was assassinated). From the transposition of the *Spera Mundi*, the armillary sphere that became his symbol, to the interpretation of his own name, *Emmanuel* ('God with us' in Hebrew), numerous 'signs' indicated that this king was God's 'Elected One', chosen to accomplish great feats. His personal political view, influenced by his schoolmaster, Diogo Rebelo, and by the Joachistic tradition (Joachim of Fiore, see p. 190) that awaited the coming of the Messiah, led him to believe that he was destined to found a new world rule, a theme that would later be taken up by Father António Vieira under the name of the Quinto Império (Fifth Empire) (see p. 64).

TRACES OF THE KABBALAH ON JERÓNIMOS MONASTERY'S SOUTH GATE

Jerónimos and the Kabbalah

Monastery of Santa Maria de Belém
Praça do Império
Tuesday to Sunday, 9.30am–5.30pm (October to June), 9.30am–6pm (July to September)
Tram 15E

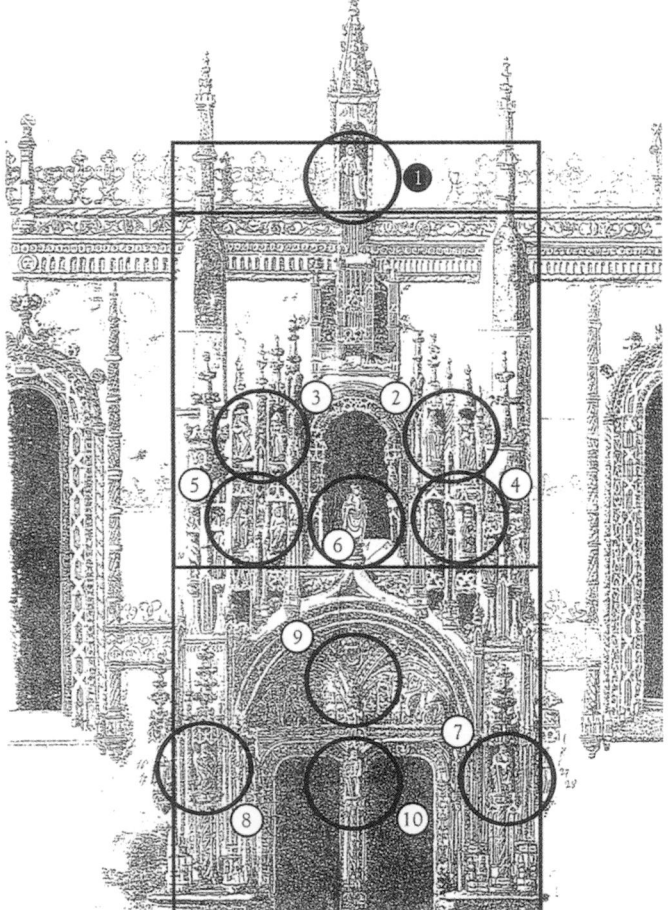

In the esoteric Judaeo-Christian tradition, the Kabbalah is the way to understanding and man's spiritual realisation in God, by following a path in the Tree of Life, which is endowed with ten divine attributes, called 'spheres' or sephirot (see p. 185).

This tree, which represents the reciprocal path of communication between God and the community of man (the Church), is clearly depicted on the south gate of Jerónimos monastery. It evokes the presence of divine power in the human world.

At the lower end of the central vertical line is crown prince Henrique of Sagres (10), the Inspired One, who represents the community of man. At the opposite end is the Archangel Michael (1), God's emissary. The Virgin and Child (6) act as mediators between man and God.

Here, the relation between each of the 10 sephirot and their 10 corresponding figures on the gate are explained.

1. KETHER ELION (crown of God). At the top, where Archangel Michael, God's emissary, stands. Corresponds to Metraton, the intermediary between Heaven and Earth.

2. CHOKMAH (wisdom) and 3. BINAH (understanding). Correspond to the Fathers and Doctors of the Church.

4. CHESOD (mercy) and 5. GEBURAH (strength, fear). Correspond to the prophets and the Sybils or, in other words, the time before the coming of Christ.

6. TIPHARETH (beauty). At the centre of the image is the Virgem Nossa Senhora dos Reis Magos (Virgin Our Lady of the Magi).

7. NETZACH (victory, God's passive resistance) and 8. HOD (splendour, God's active force). Belong entirely to the ethic of the martyr and the evangelisation of Christ's apostles.

9. YESOD (foundation). Dominated by the young Saint Sebastian, the representation of the hidden soul (see p. 123).

10. MALKUTH (kingdom). This sephirah, the kingdom of God on Earth, is represented by crown prince Dom Henrique, the Inspired One, who holds the privileged status of being the representative of the community of man before God. He also incarnates the feminine nature of the *Shekinah* (Holy Spirit). Henrique was a momentary divine incarnation and was at the origin of the early period of the great maritime discoveries.

For more on the Kabbalah, see the following double-page spread.

To learn more about the crown prince Henrique, the Inspired One, see p. 186.

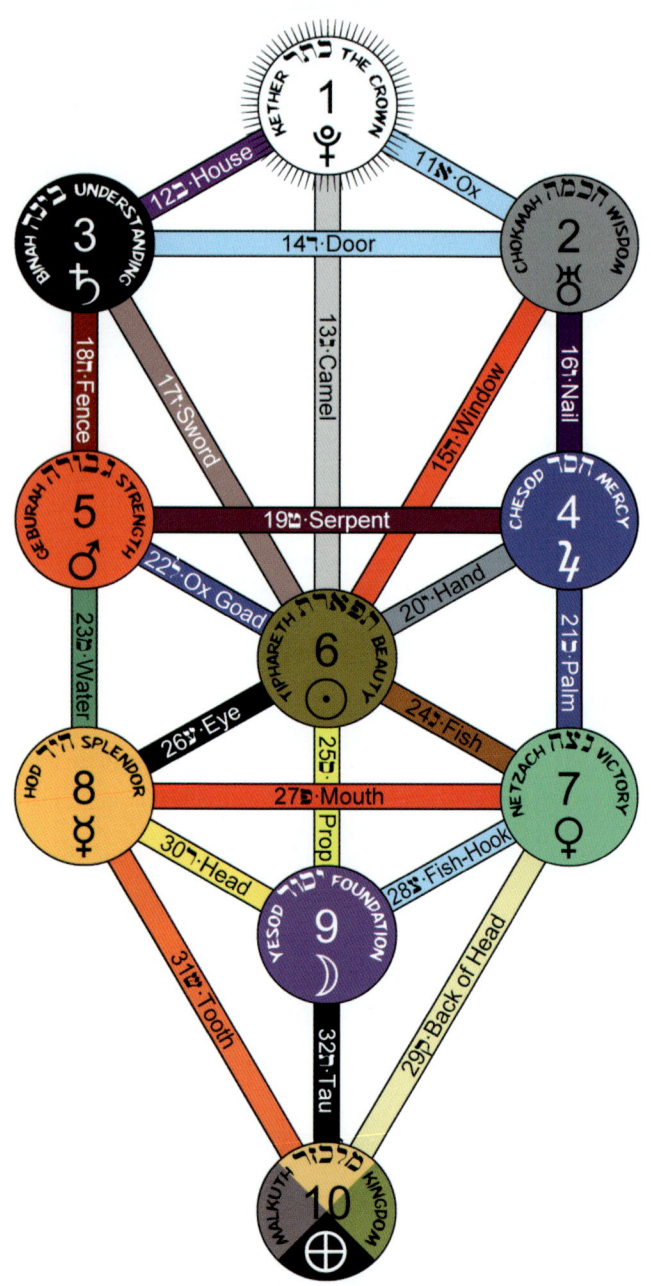

- 184 -

The Iberian kabbalah

The origin of the Kabbalah (*Tradition* in Hebrew) goes back to the dawn of time. After their flight from Egypt, led by Moses, the Hebrew people are believed to have inherited this secret, esoteric knowledge from Egyptian sages and to have adapted it to their monotheistic beliefs. Since the Pharisees and the Sadducees had strayed from the correct understanding of the Pentateuch compiled in the Talmud, a new current of thought, that of the Essenes, appeared. They became the faithful keepers of the Kabbalah's wisdom until the arrival of Jesus Christ, who immediately incorporated it into his philosophy. After Christ, the Christian gnostics of Alexandria assimilated the Judaic Kabbalah to adapt it to their own concept of the universe and of man. The Judaeo-Christian Kabbalah was born. In the 12th century, in his great work *Sepher ha-Zohar* (*Book of Splendour*), Rabbi Moses de León retranscribed the idea of the Kabbalah. Written in León but conceived in Lisbon, this work, along with the *Sepher ha-Yetzirah* (*Book of Creation*) dating from the 3rd century AD, forms the Kabbalistic system. Its origins go back to the *Maaseh Merkavah*, the first mystic Jewish system that interpreted the sacred texts of the Torah in the 1st century AD and created a new doctrine that, at first, was only transmitted orally (*shebeal pe*) by its followers (*iordei merkavah*).

In the *Sepher ha-Yetzirah*, which discusses the Universe and the laws that rule it, the patriarch Abraham reveals the understanding of Nature and its manifestations as emanations of God. The various levels of creation form ten interconnected spheres (*sephirot*) representing the paths of Kabbalistic spiritual realisation, which thus form the Tree of Life (*Otz Chaim*). The Spirit becoming the Word or Gospel is the first sphere and the breath that results from it, the second. The breath, by combining letters, gives birth to the other spheres. The third is that of water, which produces the Earth and matter. The fourth sphere is that of fire, which nourishes life. The last six spheres correspond to the four cardinal directions and the two poles. Contrary to the Rabbinical Kabbalah attributed to Isaac Luria, a Jerusalem native, the Iberian Sephardim practised Prophetic Kabbalah. Attributed to Abraham Abulafia (AD 1200), Prophetic Kabbalah is at the origin of Spanish millenarianism,* Portuguese Sebastianism,** and other Luso-European gnostic currents of thought, such as the 16th-century Master Builders and Portuguese Freemasonry at the dawn of the 19th century.

* *Spanish millenarianism: an apocalyptic doctrine about the End of Time and the coming of the universal Messiah.*
**Portuguese Sebastianism: an apocalyptic doctrine about the coming of the Messiah as the king of Portugal.*

Dom Henrique: an initiate who used the treasure of the templars to finance great discoveries

The son of King João I and Queen Dona Filipa de Lancaster, crown prince Dom Henrique of Burgundy and Lancaster was born in Porto in 1394 and lived in Viseu and Tomar for many years. It was in the Algarve, during a memorable voyage to Lagos and Sagres, that he developed his project of maritime expansion, the effects of which are still felt today. He died on 13 November 1460 and his body was transported to Santa Maria de Lagos church, which, at the time, was the seat of the *Confraria do Compromisso* (Brotherhood of Commitment). Over a month later, in 1461, on the orders of his uncle, King Dom Afonso V, the prince's mortal remains were transferred to the Santa Maria da Vitória monastery, generally known as Batalha. Diogo Gomes, a nobleman who had been present at the prince's death, told of the event and affirmed that Dom Henrique's body had not suffered any physical alterations, nearly two months after his death.

An imposing figure in Portuguese history 'enlightened by the Holy Spirit, born and raised in divine mystery', according to his chronicler Gomes Eanes de Zurara (1410-1474), crown prince Dom Henrique of Burgundy (Henry the Navigator) was indisputably the mastermind and grand architect of what would later be called the maritime epic of the 'Gesta Henriquina'. He incarnates the spiritual prerogatives of the Holy Spirit, or in other words the Third Person of the Holy Trinity called *Shiva* or *Siva* in the East, the anagram of *Avis*, the dynasty of which he was the most illustrious representative.

Dom Henrique was the supreme and secret master of the mysterious, but sovereign, Order of Mariz (*Allath-Marid*), the eighth Grand Master and administrator of the Military Order of the Knights of Christ, and the founder of the British Order of the Garter in the city of Tomar, which served as a model to the British Order of Cardo, both of which had Saint George as patron. As for Dom Henrique, he chose the Divine Holy Spirit as his patron saint. We have Dom Henrique to thank for the Hebrew translation of the book *Segredo dos Segredos de Astrologia* (*Secret of the Secrets of Astrology*), a treatise based on Aristotelian philosophy but that also explained Kabbalistic astrology. The book was heavily consulted by the sailors of the Naval Academy of Sagres. Indeed, it was thanks to their knowledge of astrology and astronomy, based on the position of the stars, that they traced their maritime routes.

The final administrator of the purported 'Treasure of the Temple', Dom Henrique used wealth inherited from the former Knights Templar to finance the great discoveries. He was also a great academic, carrying out profound reforms of the University of Lisbon. To the disciplines that already existed at the beginning of the 15th century (Law – Decrees – Grammar – Logic – Physics – Philosophy – Theology – Music), Dom Henrique added Medicine, Natural and Moral Philosophy, Arithmetic, Geometry and Astrology in 1431. Zurara, the biographer of crown prince Henrique of Sagres, was an educated man with an interest in the occult sciences of the Kabbalah and in astrology, as his chronicles prove. The likeliness of his being a 'New Christian' (converted Jew) is revealed in his *Chronicle of the Discovery* and *Conquest of Guinea*, in which he examined the horoscope of the illustrious prince and

wrote: 'However, I want to tell you here how, yet again because of a natural influence, this honoured Prince had an interest for all these [esoteric] things. And that because he was an Aries ascendant, which is in the house of Mars, and the exaltation of the Sun. Given that the aforementioned Mars was in Aquarius, which is in the house of Saturn, and in the house of Hope, that meant that this Lord strived towards heroic and strong conquests, in particular to search for things that were hidden from other men, and secretive, according to the quality of Saturn, in whose house he is. And because he is accompanied by the Sun, as I said, and the Sun is in the house of Jupiter, that meant that all these treaties and conquests would be carried out loyally, and with the pleasure of your King and Lord.'

SYMBOLS OF THE CELL DOORS OF HIERONYMITE MONKS ③

The Hieronymites and Joachim of Fiore's three ages of the world

Monastery of Santa Maria de Belém
Praça do Império
Tuesday to Sunday, 9.30am–5.30pm (October to June), 9.30am–6pm (July to September)
Tram 15E

The cells of the monks of the Order of Saint Jerome, or the Hieronymites (Jerónimos), of the Santa Maria de Belém Monastery were connected to the cloister and to the interior of the church. Striking symbols on the doors of these cramped rooms can still be seen today.

The Hieronymite religious order, founded in Italy in 1377, is an evolution of the movement led by Tommasucio da Duccio (a member of the Third Order of Saint Francis of Assisi in his earlier days) towards the inspired spirituality of the Fathers of the Desert, to which Saint Jerome belonged.

The spirituality of the monks of the order was centred on mental prayers on Christ's wisdom, as Saint Jerome had practised. The Hieronymites followed the messianic and millenarian theories of the Fraticelli Franciscans, inspired by Joachim of Fiore, the author of the three ages of the world concept (see following double page). The last of these three ages, that of the Holy Spirit, was represented by Emmanuel, with whom Dom Manuel I shared his name, which partly explains why he offered this monastery to the Hieronymites who, as a result, came from Penha Longa de Sintra to settle here.

A sculpted Janus or Tricephalous Christ can be found on one of the cells. It symbolises the three ages of the world: the Past for the Father and Adam (associated with Jerusalem); the Present for the Son and Christ (Rome); and the Future for the Holy Spirit and Saint Benedict (Joachim of Fiore was a Cistercian, and thus also Benedictine) (Lisbon).

This concept is repeated in other compositions such as that of the three dogs, representing the guardians of the universal Church (*domini-canes*, dogs of the Lord or, in other words, the guardians of traditional Wisdom), or that of the three principles of alchemy: Sulphur, for the Spirit and the Father (an eagle on a Moor's head); Mercury, for the Soul and the Son (a head crowned with two angels, symbols of the winged androgyne); and Salt, for the Body and the Holy Spirit (a winged dragon with a three-horned baphometic head). Silver is represented by a crowned queen and Gold by the crowned Mercury.

Etymologically, Jerónimo or Hierónimo comes from *Hiero-Manas*, meaning 'inspired Spirit' or 'universal Wisdom'.

Joachim of Fiore and the three ages of the world

Joachim of Fiore (Gioacchino da Fiore) was born in Celico, Cosenza in Calabra province, Italy, around 1132, and died in 1202 in the small abbey of San Martino de Canele, in Calabra. His remains were transferred to the abbey of San Giovanni in Fiore. The son of Maurus of Celico, a notary in the service of the Norman kings of Sicily, Joachim grew up at court, but his religious vocation led him on a pilgrimage to the Holy Land to deepen his faith, which was prey to an intense mysticism. Legend says that, during Lent, while in contemplation before Mount Tabor, he had a vision and received the divine inspiration that would guide him all his life. Back in Italy, he became a Benedictine monk at the abbey of Corazzo and was ordained a priest. He thus consecrated his time exclusively to biblical study, searching for the profound meaning of the Holy Scriptures. Because of his reputation for virtue and wisdom, he was elected to become abbot, but he sought an exemption from Pope Lucius III who freed him from his functions in 1182 so he could concentrate on his research. In the following years, he worked on his books at the abbey of Casamari, assisted by Luca Campano, a young monk who would later become the archbishop of Cosenza. Increasingly focused on his work, Joachim of Fiore withdrew to the hermitage of Pietralata and founded Fiore Abbey in the Calabrian mountains.

This abbey became the centre of a new independent order, nevertheless based on the Benedictine rule and statutes of the Cistercian order, but with more rigour and mysticism. The followers of this new order were called the Joaquimitas or Florians, in honour of its founder. At his death, Fiore's saintly reputation led him to be venerated as such, even though he was never officially beatified. During his lifetime, he was considered to be a 'prophetic, inspired' man. The revolutionary character of his apocalyptic and prophetic thought mainly targeted the reform of the Church, for which he could count on wide support. It is rather surprising, in fact, that many Florian ideas that were condemned by the Lateran Council of 1215 were implicitly accepted by the Franciscans and eminent members of the clergy, even if they denounced the worldly and capitalistic aspects in which they participated. The thinking of Joachim of Fiore is expressed in three principle works: *Psalterium decem chordarum* (Psaltery of Ten Strings), *Liber concordie Novi ac Veteris Testamenti* (Book of Harmony of the New and Old Testaments) and *Expositio in Apocalypsim* (Exposition of the Apocalypse). He wrote about the history of humanity (diverging from time to time with calculations and analogies to events recounted in the Old Testament), identified the connections to the New Testament, and divided history into three distinct ages: 1) the age of the Father, which begins with Adam and ends with Christ, making a total of 1260 years recounted in the Old Testament; 2) the age of the Son, also lasting about 1260 years (which was meant to allow mystics to later adapt the date of the beginning of the Third Age) and described in the New Testament; and 3) the age of the Holy Spirit, which begins with the defeat of the antichrist, and whose sacred text, the *Eternal Gospel*, would be the fusion of the two previous texts (Old and New Testaments) leading to a period of universal Brotherhood in which Christians, Jews and Arabs would live in peace in a spiritualised atmosphere. It would be the quintessential Age of monks (priests), but the secular would not be excluded.

Each age was to last 40 generations and be announced by a precursor. Osias had been the precursor of the second age begun by Zachary, father of John the Baptist. Saint Benedict was the precursor of the third age. The first age was the age of subservience, characterised by fear, and that of marriage (the married priests of the Old Testament). The second was the age of filial obedience, characterised by faith, and that of the priesthood. The third would be the age of liberty, characterised by charity, and that of monasticism. The *Eternal Gospel* is supposedly the book mentioned by Saint John in Revelation 14:6: 'Then I saw another angel flying in the midst of heaven, having the everlasting gospel to preach to those who dwell on the earth, to every nation, tribe, tongue, and people.' With this brief summary it is possible to imagine the impact that Joachim of Fiore's ideas had on his followers. Later, the Franciscans adopted them and were quickly won over to the representatives of the Third Age, of which Saint Francis of Assisi became the herald. His ideas rapidly spread to southern Italy, from Sicily to Provence (where they appeared in the *Lais d'amour* and the *Romance of the Rose*, in the part written by Jean de Meug), to Aragon (through Arnado de Vilanova and Raimundo Lúlio) and to Portugal (by the Holy Roman Empress Isabelle). Later, the influence of the idea of the Coming is clearly seen in the religious orthodoxy of the Jesuits. It was at this time that the inspired thought of the Jesuit António Vieira appeared. He added two additional ages to those of Fiore, one linked to Sebastian the King and another to Sebastian the Saint.

Vera IOACCHIN Praeclari est quâ cernnis imago
Qui vult, atque animo mirus in orbe fuit.

Alchemy and the religious order
of the Middle Ages and the Renaissance

Most religious orders of the Middle Ages and the Renaissance considered Alchemy (from the Coptic term *Allah-Chemia*, or divine chemistry) as the Art of the Holy Spirit or Royal Art of the divine creation of the world and man. It was connected to Orthodox Catholic doctrine.

The followers of this Art divided it into two principal forms. Spiritual alchemy exclusively concerns the Inspiration of the soul, transforming the impure elements of the body in the refined states of spiritual consciousness, which is also called the Way of the Repentants. Laboratory alchemy, called the Way of the Philosophers, reproduces the alchemical universe of the transmutation of nature's impure elements into noble metals, such as silver and gold, in the laboratory. These two alchemical practices are generally followed in combination, thus becoming the Way of the Humble, where the humility is that of man faced with the grandeur of the universe reproduced in the laboratory (in Latin *labor + oratorium*); the alchemy of the (interior) soul is expressed exteriorly in the laboratory. Those who practice Laboratory alchemy with the sole purpose of finding silver and gold, and thus neglect the essential aspects of the betterment of the Soul, will fail and become charlatans, who might have a wide-ranging culture but certainly not the required moral qualities. To avoid becoming a charlatan (it was this heretic form that was condemned by the Church), followers must balance the heart and soul, culture and moral qualities, penitence and humility, to become a true philosopher.

The alchemy tradition has left a number of traces in Portugal, such as at the Convento de Cristo in Tomar where *Espagíria*, the fabrication of natural elixirs or medicines to help the needy, was practised. This practice was also carried out at the Convento dos Capuchos da Serra de Sintra and the Convento de São Diniz de Odivelas, where Dona Feliciana de Milão (1642-1705) wrote her *Discourse on the Philosopher's Stone*. At Lisbon's Convento do Carmo the decorated tomb of an alchemist surrounded by the instruments of his art can also be seen.

Ancient documents show that several alchemists passed through Lisbon, including Raimuno Lúlio, Arnaldo de Vilanova and Paracelse. Some Portuguese alchemists became known as early as the 13th century, such as Pedro Hispano (the only Portuguese pope, John XXI) who corresponded with Albert the Great and his disciple, Thomas Aquinas, who wrote the only alchemical treatise on water, *Tractatus Mirabilis Aquarium*. In the 15th century, King Dom Afonso V of Portugal wrote a treatise on the Philosopher's Stone in two parts: *Lapis Philosophorum* and *Divisão dos quatro elementos* (Division of the Four Elements). In 1556, the Inquisition accused Father António de Gouveia, a native of the Azores, of practicing alchemy and of knowing how to transform lead into gold. Monk Frei Vicente Nogueira saw his entire library of alchemical texts burnt to the ground by the Inquisition. In the 17th century, the Portuguese mathematician Pedro Nunes corresponded with English alchemist John Dee, and Duarte Madeira Arrais wrote the alchemical treatise *Novae Philosophiae*. In the 18th century, King Dom João V encouraged the publication of the alchemical works of Raphael Bluteau, deservedly nicknamed the 'Lusitanian Hermes'. Anselmo Caetano Munhoz de Abreu e Castelo Branco also published his famous work dedicated to Dom João V, *Ennoea ou Aplicação do Entendimento sobre a Pedra Filosofal* (*Application of Knowledge on the Philosopher's Stone*). In 1724, a book of alchemical images, without any captions, also known as a *liber mutus*, or mute book, was published; it belonged to the library of King Dom Carlos. Finally, towards the end of the 19th century and during the first quarter of the 20th century, the Portuguese-Brazilian António Augusto Carvalho Monteiro suddenly appeared, leaving his property Quinta da Regaleira in Sintra. This is currently the largest building in Portugal containing alchemical elements associated with the Catholic gnosis. This unique site is thus a veritable *Roseiral Mariano* (philosophers' rose garden), the name given by the ancients to alchemical treatises, regardless of their form, whether written, drawn, painted or sculpted.

CHÃO SALGADO

④

Reminder of the scandal caused by a faked assassination attempt

Beco do Chão Salgado – Belém – Tram 15E

Behind the famous Pastéis de Belém bakery is the *Beco do Chão Salgado* (Salted Earth Alley), a place that most Lisbon residents have forgotten about but that is linked to a terrible event of Portuguese history that shocked all of civilised Europe in the 18th century. As part of the conservative nobility and traditional clergy, represented by the Jesuits, were opposed to his social reforms, the Marquis of Pombal tried to neutralise them. It is said that he went so far as to fake an assassination of King Dom José I on 3 September 1758, and to accuse the Távora family of the crime. This family, which was closely linked to the Jesuits, constituted the main opposition to the enlightened despot. The attack took place not far from here, near the palace of Dom José de Mascarenhas, duke of Aveiro, which was quite opportune as he was the most distinguished member of the Távora family. Although the Távora family denied all accusations, they were condemned to death, their possessions were confiscated by the Crown, their name was erased from noble lineage and their familial coat of arms smashed to pieces. From that point on, it was forbidden to mention their name. The intervention of Queen Mariana and Dona Maria Francisca finally saved most of the family, to the great annoyance of the Marquis of Pombal. As for the Marquise of Távora, she was not spared. Along with the four other family members accused and sentenced to death, she was tortured and executed in public on 13 January 1759, nearby in front of what is now the palace of the president of the Republic. The execution reached unheard-of degrees of savagery. The bones of the hands and feet of the condemned, who were decapitated, were broken with clubs, and the rest of the bodies were burned and their ashes thrown in the Tagus. Making the most of the occasion, the event was used to throw the Jesuits out of the kingdom. The duke of Aveiro's palace was also demolished and salt was poured on the ground, a punishment ordered by the Marquis of Pombal so that nothing would ever grow there again. Yet the same year, Dom José I had a stone monument to the family erected. It displays five sculpted rings, one for each executed member of the Távora family. At its base, a funerary stele recounts the event.

SIGNS OF THE PORTUGUESE WORLD EXHIBITION

Fascinating forgotten traces of an exhibition from 1940

Belém Tropical Botanical Garden, Largo dos Jerónimos
213 616 340 – museus.ulisboa.pt/jardim-botanico-tropical
Tram 15E

Inaugurated in 1906 by King Dom Carlos I, the Belém Tropical Botanical Garden covers an area of seven hectares and is home to more than 600 tropical species. The garden is in a precarious condition, despite the start of a restoration campaign, but allows for a walk out of time to discover the surprising traces of the Exposition of the Portuguese World

(Exposição do Mundo Português) that took place in the Belém district during the Second World War, between 23 June and 2 September 1940.

A veritable propaganda organ of the Estado Novo (1937–1945), the exhibition was intended to commemorate the 800th anniversary of the official foundation of the Portuguese State (1140) and the 300th anniversary of the reconquest of independence (1640). Although most of what had been built for the occasion was destroyed, three works survived: the garden of the Praça do Império, the famous Monument of the Discoveries and the building that now houses the Museum of Popular Art.

Less well known still are the fascinating traces of the exhibition that can be found here and there in the garden, i.e. where the colonial section used to be: the Casa Colonial (today Casa da Direção) with its beautiful azulejos with images of the colonies, the old colonial restaurant, as well as the Raw Materials Pavilion, the Macao Arch and the Moon Gate.

Scattered around the park, the 14 African and Asian busts by sculptor Manuel de Oliveira also date from the years of the exhibition.

Two wooden panels by sculptor Alípio Brandão, depicting the themes of agriculture and fishing in the colonies, were also part of the exhibition and are now kept in the nearby Palais da Calheta (closed to the public).

The place where Luis de Camões is said to have written Os Lusiadas

To the west of the garden, next to the Macao arch, there are carps and turtles, plants endemic to China, the Bridge of the Nine curves, some benches, the small Chinese Pavilion, but also a miniature replica of the cave of Luis de Camões, introduced by the Macao Foundation on the occasion of the 1998 Lisbon Expo. According to legend, it was in this garden that the poet wrote the most important work of Portuguese literature, *Os Lusiadas*. The bust to the east is a replica of the one made by sculptor Bordalo Pinheiro (1866) in China.

THE TOMB OF THE MARQUIS OF POMBAL

The posthumous adventures of the Marquis of Pombal

Igreja da Senhora do Livramento e São José
Largo da Memória, Freguesia da Ajuda
Monday to Saturday, 3pm to 7pm
Visit by reservation: 213635295

The mortal remains of Sebastião José de Carvalho e Mello, the famous and controversial Marquis of Pombal (see p. 249), are in Ajuda, in an urn kept in the church of the Senhora do Livramento e São José (Our Lady of Deliverance and Saint Joseph). This neoclassical Lisbon monument was built in 1760, two years after the Távora family episode. King Dom José I had it built to commemorate the fact that he escaped the assassination attempt carried out against him at this spot. It is now known as the Igreja da Memória (Memory church). Sebastião José passed away in Pombal and was initially buried on 8 May 1782, dressed in his Franciscan habit and the insignias of the Order of Christ, in the church of the São Francisco de Nossa Senhora do Cardel convent. During the third French invasion of Portugal (1807), the convent was

used as a barracks and the tomb was desecrated by soldiers hoping to find valuable objects.

Despite the intervention of General Massena, the soldiers left the bones on the church floor. In 1856, Marshal Saldanha ordered the transfer of the remains to Lisbon, while the empty coffin remained as a 'relic' in Pombal. The mortal remains of the Marquis of Pombal were placed in an abandoned tomb reposing on four carved elephants in the *Mercês* (Graces) chapel, on rua do Século (Century), where he had been baptised on 6 June 1699. When the decision was made to demolish this chapel in the 20th century, the tomb and remains were to be disposed of along with the rest of the sacristy, but on 7 November 1910, Lisbon's Municipal Board added them to its archives. It was not until 1923 that they were transferred to this church of Memory, on the initiative of the fifth Marquis of Pombal and a Republican commission presided over by Borges Grainha, a Freemason.

The church was closed until 23 December 1951, when a group of soldiers from the 7th Cavalry Regiment reopened it for worship on their own initiative. It had to be closed again in 1985 when lightning seriously damaged its dome.

Thanks to recent renovations, the church and the Marquis of Pombal's mausoleum is now open to the public (advance booking required).

THE MYSTERIOUS FOUNTAIN WITH FORTY SPOUTS

A pair of entwined snakes representing the perfect union of masculine and feminine

Calçada da Ajuda
Daily, 10am–5pm (Octobre and November), 10am–6pm (May to October)
Tram 18E

Dating from the 18th century, the Fountain of the Forty Spouts (*Fonte das 40 Bicas*) in the Ajuda Botanical Garden is also known as the Fountain of the Snakes. It is decorated with a mythological statue of Neptune, Greek god of the oceans, and with other pieces, such as the dolphins adorning both front and side sections, the seahorses seated on the upper part and the detached snakes, two of which are entwined, back-to-back. These surround the upper platform and give birth to a number of reptiles coiled around trunks of dead wood – all of which is in line with the hermeticism of the Pombaline era.

Symbolically, the sinuous movements of the telluric currents that run through the earth and its water tables (a great many of which are brought to the surface thanks to monumental fountains such as that in the botanical garden) have long been associated with the snake. By virtue of its telluric connection inside the earth, the snake has also become the symbol of the 'wisdom of the depths', revealed by the Water of Life gushing at the surface.

The two intertwined snakes, situated at the front of the fountain, embody the union of male and female natures, leading to a third state of perfection, that of androgyny, in which the individual achieves a perfect synthesis of male and female elements. This is an obvious reference to the episode drawn from Greek mythology describing how the blind prophet Tiresias of Thebes encountered two snakes engaged in the act of mating. He struck them with his stick, killed the female and found himself immediately transformed into a woman. Seven years later, 'he' came across another pair of snakes copulating. He killed the male and was changed back into a man, but this time with the gift of sight since he had achieved a state of inner enlightenment, thus granting him the immortality of the perfect androgyne.

A little further to the front, facing the entwined pair, there is a third snake, on its own, coiled up and with its head raised. It represents the Primordial Ocean of the Waters of Life. This cobra is in fact a Naja, a metaphor for monarchy and an animal sacred to the Hindus. Finally, at the apex of the fountain there are various seahorses, which, as they share in the secret of the fertilising waters, know the path that they are travelling. For this reason, they were said to possess the gift of being able to create springs at will.

The purpose of Neptune's ascent is to stimulate the imagination, or 'creative spirit': this is evoked by the flying fish rising upwards among the four seahorses. The frogs on the second platform show the way to gradual knowledge.

THE *POMPEIA* ROOM
OF PALÁCIO DA EGA

Forgotten marvels

Freguesia de Alcântara
Calçada da Boa-Hora, 30
Free guided tour by reservation (Instituto de Investigaçao Científica Tropical:
213 616 330)
Tram 15E

Hidden behind Ega Moniz hospital, the Pátio do Saldanha palace, better known as Palácio da Ega, contains part of Lisbon's lost history. To visit this splendid 16th-century palace, take the calçada da Boa-Hora (Right-Time road), where the Overseas Historic Archives are now located.

Surrounded by a beautiful garden embellished with a large lake, the building bears the coat of arms of the Coutinho, Albuquerque and Saldanha families on its central gate.

Inside is the magnificent Pompeia room, dating from the beginning of the 18th century, also called the 'music room', 'column room' or 'room of the marshals'. Especially notable are the statue of the god of music, the magnificent columns, the dome, and the frescoes on the walls, as well as the eight 18th-century azulejo panels depicting Europe's main ports, the work of Dutch artist Boumeester.

The room's current design dates from the 19th century, when it was entirely remodelled. The original wooden ceiling was removed, the upper windows were filled in, and a false dome resting on eight hollow wooden columns was constructed. The panels were also repainted in the style of the period, leaving the original azulejos untouched.

The most famous resident and owner of this palace was the Countess of Ega, Dona Juliana Maria Luisa Carolina Sofia de Oyenhausen e Almeida, who, in 1795, wed the second count of Ega (the name of a village near Coimbra), Aires José Maria de Saldanha. The countess was a very beautiful woman and had several famous lovers, including General Junot and Marshal Beresford.

The origin of Stroganoff

After the count's death, the Countess of Ega remarried. Her new husband was the Count of Stroganoff, a Russian from Saint Petersburg, the city where she would die in 1827. During her time there, she discovered a recipe from the count's chef that later became famous in Portugal. By browning beef, tomatoes and mushrooms in a casserole, then adding sour cream, it is easy to make Stroganoff, to be served with rice.

THE ROTUNDA
OF SANTO AMARO CHAPEL

When in danger of drowning ...

Alto de Santo Amaro – Tram 15E
Saturday and Sunday during mass (9am and 7pm)

The stunning Saint Maurus chapel (*Santo Amaro*), founded in 1549, is located in Alto de Santo Amaro de Alcântara, on a hill with a superb view of part of the city and the Tagus. The legend depicted on the polychrome azulejo panels that cover the interior tells of a Galician ship on the verge of being wrecked.

The crew cried out to Saint Maurus, praying to be saved, and the ship was miraculously able to reach the shore at this part of the river. To thank Heaven, they founded this chapel. Another, more plausible, version says that the chapel was founded by 14 monks of the Ordem de Cristo (Order of Christ) after their return from Rome, where they had gone in pilgrimage to the basilica of Saint John Lateran. When their boat passed by on the Tagus, they noticed this spot and chose it as the place where they would dedicate their lives to asceticism. On 15 January 1532, they founded the

Brotherhood of Saint Maurus, the saint to evoke when in danger of drowning.

The brotherhood received numerous honours and privileges from the pope and different Portuguese kings. Connected to Saint John Lateran, the brotherhood was made up exclusively of nobles, such as the Count of Sabugosa, who was still its clerk when it was abolished in 1836. The feasts of 15 January, in honour of Saint Maurus, were celebrated enthusiastically and were full of life and colour thanks to the participation of the Galicians, the traditional water-carriers of Lisbon. This circular chapel has a rather curious polygonal layout, with seven straight sides, four of which are closed while the other three are open and thus form the doors to the church, also circular in form. This creates a sort of 'ambulatory' (charola or rotunda) like that found in the Freires de Cristo convent at Tomar, which is itself inspired by the octagonal design of the São Gregório Nazianzeno chapel of Santa Maria do Olival located in the same city.

A section of the azulejo panels near the side altar depicts Saint Maurus, dressed as a pilgrim, leaning on a rod and carrying the Book of Hours. This saint, abbot and bishop is the champion of those suffering from broken arms or legs because, when he was alive, he had the miraculous power of healing broken bones. This was perhaps also an allusion to his missionary work, in the sense that he rectified deviations to the original doctrine just as he realigned bones. This explains why the ambulatory is decorated with arm and leg motifs, also found on the azulejos of the step leading to the main altar.

For more information about the charola, see following double-page.

Who was Saint Maurus?

Maurus of Glanfeuil (feast day 15 January) is believed to have been born in Rome in AD 510 and to have died in Glanfeuil (Anjou) in 584. Along with Saint Benedict of Nursia – of whom he was the closest disciple – he is believed to have founded the abbey of Monte Cassino (Italy) in 528. He introduced the Order of Saint Benedict to Gaul by founding the Glanfeuil monastery, where he taught agriculture to peasants. As a result, he is the patron saint of farmers to this day.

In the 17th century, his name was given to a reformed Benedictine congregation. Among his numerous miracles, one of the best known is when he saved a fellow monk, Placidus, who was drowning in Subiaco lake with no one nearby to save him. Saint Benedict had a vision of this danger and ordered Saint Maurus to go and save the young monk. He walked on the water, took hold of his fellow monk by the hair, and saved him from imminent death. Saint Maurus is also venerated because he heals arthritic and rheumatic pains, as well as headaches. Iconographically, he is shown wearing a monk's hood and holding a crozier and a crutch.

Mystery of the ambulatory of the knights templar

It is fairly certain that the Order of Christ built the ambulatory of the Santo Amaro d'Alcântara hermitage with the purpose of reproducing west of Lisbon the Great Ambulatory (*Grande Charola*) that it had built in Tomar. Dom Gualdim Pais, the master of the Portuguese Templars, commissioned the construction of the Tomar convent ambulatory from the Builder-Monks of the Cistercian Order on 1 March 1160. It was to be the exact replica of the Mosque of Omar and the Church of the Holy Sepulchre, two round constructions on the site of the ancient Temple of Solomon in Jerusalem. The purpose of building the Tomar ambulatory was to create a new Temple of Jerusalem at the head of the Iberian peninsula to synthesise the West and the traditionalism of the East. The three religions of the Book (Judaism, Christianity and Islam) would thus be united in a single Temple, that of the true, unique God, in concordance with the theory of the transfer of power (*translatio imperii*). Originally, the oratory of the Knights Templar stood here. Based on the classic form of Syrian mosques, it was a very simple construction. However, in 1356, when Tomar became the seat of the Order of Christ (on the suppression of the Knights Templar), Prince Dom Henrique (see p. 186) had the ambulatory modified and enhanced in order to adapt it to the functions of the new convent of the Order of Christ and to make it the apse of the Order's church. Most of the paintings and frescoes (almost exclusively biblical scenes) date from

the 16th century, as do the golden statues below the Byzantine dome.

The interior of the ambulatory is octagonal in shape (the centre has eight sides), while the exterior walls are composed of – or, more precisely, were once composed of – sixteen sides reinforced by solid buttresses (two side sections were removed when the church was enlarged in the 16th century during the Manueline period).

In this drawing of the ambulatory, or charola –

a word that reflects its circular form, like the related French term *carole*, meaning a circle, or dance in the round (as in rotunda, another word for a round building) – we find the octagon and the number eight reflected in the number of sides. The medieval symbolism of both is fully adapted to the original functions of the oratory and the apse

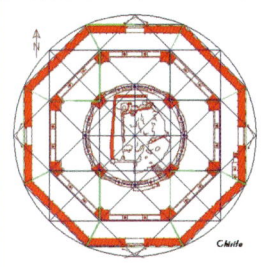

of the ambulatory. Considered as the place of passage from mortality to immortality, it served as a psychopomp (guide of souls) or as the intermediary between the two worlds, the visible and the invisible, and hence represented the Arch of the Alliance of God and Humanity. In the Middle Ages, the octagon was the intermediary shape between the square (the Earth) and the circle (the Heavens) and was the spiritual symbol of passage, that is of Christ's resurrection and of the beginning of human perfection. The octagon thus expresses Divine Power in the mortal world, represented by the manifestation of Heavenly Jerusalem on Earth, in this case the ambulatory.

The Kabbalistic meaning of the number eight further reinforces the symbolic significance of the octagon as it holds the double square of the Earth and of Man in balance. In the Christian tradition, the number eight is the number of Redemption and Prosperity.

Eight is also one more than seven, or, in other words, one more than Plenitude. Christ exceeded the Jewish Plenitude (the number seven) in his resurrection on the dawn of the eighth day.

The eighth day became the first day (the day of the Lord, *Dominica dies*), Sunday, in opposition to Saturday (*Shabbat*), or rest, the seventh day when the Lord rested after his Work of Creation. This is why the most important Christian celebrations (Easter and Christmas) last eight days. They are celebrated for eight days, with the second Sunday being the extension of the celebration. The eighth day, the day of the Resurrection, connects Christians, through baptism, to the paschal mystery of Jesus Christ (the octagonal form is often found in the design of baptismal fonts). In Roman art, the eight-pointed star (one square superposed over another at an angle, a symbol of spiritual transformation) and the eight-petalled rosette have the same significance.

To learn more about the importance of octagons, see the following double-page.

The five basic solids and sacred geometry

Sacred geometry is a world vision according to which the basic criteria for existence are perceived as being sacred. Through them can be contemplated the *Magnum Misterium*, the Universal Grand Project, by learning its laws, principles and the inter-relationships of shapes. These universal shapes are systematised in a geometric complex in which each figure has its own mathematical and philosophical interpretation. They are applied in projects of sacred architecture and sacred art, which always use the 'divine' proportions in which Man reflects the Universe, and vice versa. It is a common belief that sacred geometry and its mathematical relationships, which are harmonic and proportional, are also found in Music, Light and Cosmology. Man first discovered this system of values in prehistoric times, in the megalithic and Neolithic cultures, for example, and some consider it to be a universal facet of the human condition.

Sacred geometry is fundamental to the construction of sacred structures, such as synagogues, churches and mosques, and also plays a role in creating the interior sacred space of temples, through the altars and tabernacles. Passed down from Graeco-Egyptian culture and exported to ancient Rome, sacred geometry in the European Middle Ages inspired the creation of the Roman and Gothic architecture of Europe's medieval cathedrals, which incorporate this geometry of sacred symbolism.

It is said that Pythagoras (Samos, c. 570 BC – Metapontum, c. 497 BC) was the one who founded the system of sacred geometry in his school in Croton, Greece. This Greek philosopher and mathematician is believed to have brought the knowledge he acquired in Egypt and India back to Greece. Using the golden ratio (1.618) and applying it to the geometric forms of the five basic solids, Pythagoras created the mathematical method universally known as Pythagorean geometry.

To create the five solids (the tetrahedron or pyramid, the hexahedron or cube, the octahedron, the dodecahedron and the icosahedron), about which Plato would later philosophise (to such a point that they would become known as the five Platonic solids), Pythagoras was inspired by the Greek myth about the child-god Dionysus' toys: a basket, dice, top, ball and mirror. On a cosmic level, the basket represents the Universe; the dice, the five Platonic solids symbolising the natural elements (ether, air, fire, water, earth); the top is the atom of matter; the ball, the Earth's globe; and, finally, the mirror reflects the work of the Supreme Geometrist (Dionysus), which itself is the universal manifestation of Life and Consciousness, of God towards Man and vice versa. Each of the five Platonic solids also represents a planetary energy that is connected by its form to a natural element. Thus, the dodecahedron is traditionally linked to Venus and ether, the natural quintessence, expressed by a temple's dome. The octahedron, linked to Saturn and the air, represents the transept's cross. The tetrahedron, linked to Mars and fire, is symbolised by the openings in the temple through which light gushes forth. The icosahedron, linked to the Moon and water, establishes the harmony of forms in the temple design, constructing the connecting lines between the altars and columns. Finally, the hexahedron (cube), fixes the Sun to its element, the earth, by determining the shape of the temple's foundation or floor.

The main purpose of sacred geometry is thus to create Universal Perfection through perfect mathematical forms and calculations, and, by using sacred architecture, to connect the Multiple to the Single in a space that is geometrically dedicated to this end.

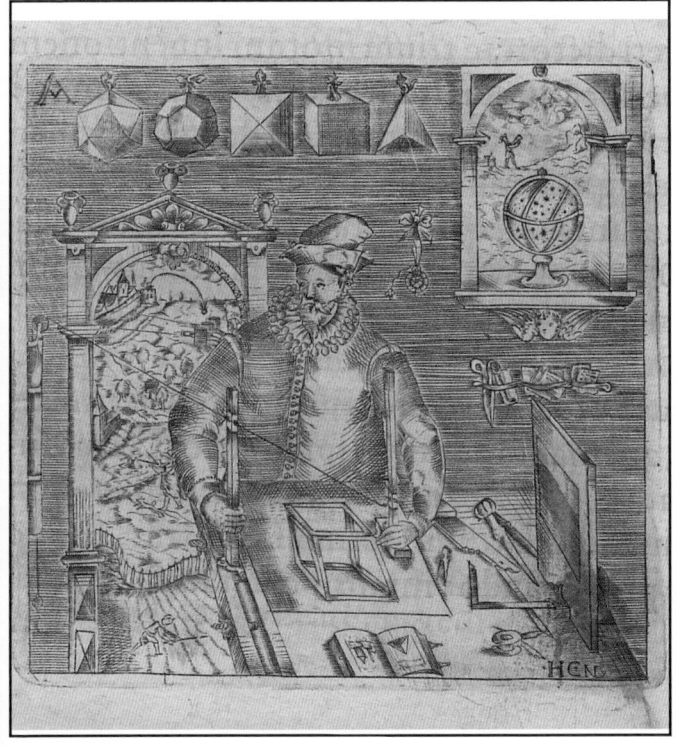

THE LISBON OBSERVATORY

A visit out of time

Tapada de Ajuda
213 921 808
geral@museus.ulisboa.pt
museus.ulisboa.pt/observatorio-astronomico-de-lisboa
Free guided tours every Wednesday afternoon in Portuguese, without
reservation
Tram18E

On Wednesday afternoons, cancel all other commitments to visit the magnificent Lisbon Observatory on the heights of Alcantara (no reservation required), set in a delightful timeless atmosphere. It was completed by King Dom Pedro V, who ceded this privileged space in the heart of his hunting ground, thus allowing Portugal to contribute to international research on the cartography of the universe and the stars. The building is in the shape of a cross, with the four points oriented according to the cardinal points, and was built between 1861 and 1867. It was inspired by the Russian Pulkovo observatory.

As well as playing an important role in the history of astronomy, the observatory signalled daylight saving time, and the return to standard time, of Portugal until 2022: all the country's clocks were in fact synchronised according to this institution.

During guided tours, you can admire a selection of the 200 objects housed here: globes of the celestial vault, the first communication machine in Morse, Portugal's first telephone, clocks and all sorts of instruments for measuring time and observing the sky, including magnificent period telescopes and their spectacular sunroofs.

It was here that Gago Coutinho came to set up his instruments to make the first seaplane flight between Portugal and Brazil. The view from the large windows on the top floor overlooking the Tagus River and the Tapadas de Ajuda, which miraculously still extend over 100 hectares of the city, is truly unmissable.

Farther away

TEMPLAR INSCRIPTIONS

Is Brigid's skull linked to the Templars' Baphomet?

Igreja de São João Baptista
Largo de São João Baptista, Lumiar
Visits when open for mass, 9am and 5pm
Metro Ameixoeira

Three largely unknown tombs are set in the lateral exterior wall of São João Baptista church in Lumiar.

One of them bears this striking inscription: 'In these tombs lie three Iberian knights who brought the head of Saint Brigid the Blessed of Hibernia (Ireland), whose relics are found in this chapel erected in her memory by the officers of this blessed Lady in January 1283.'

As the church is on Ameixoeira land, which belonged to the Order of the Knights Templar, it is not impossible for these tombs to be those of Templar knights, who illustrate, here, the Iberian myth of the three sons of the goddess Brigit (Brian, Iuchar and Uar, the spirits of inspiration who, according to Celtic mythology, collectively fathered one son – Ecne, science or poetry).

Before becoming the Christian Brigid, she was the Celtic divinity Brigit, venerated throughout Western Europe.

Her skull was brought here in 1283, on the order of the Provincial Grand Master of the Temple of Portugal, Dom Frei João Fernandes, who had close connections to king-troubadour Dom Dinis and wise king Dom Afonso de Leão e Castela.

Yet today, in the São João Bastista church of Lumiar, worshippers venerate the relic of Saint Brigid of Ireland that was supposedly brought from the monastery of São Dinis de Ovidela: a piece of her skull in an elegant urn of gilded silver in Dom João V style. For some, this skull is connected to the mythical Baphomet of the Knights Templar (see opposite).

What exactly is the Baphomet?

It is sometimes said that the Templars venerated a mysterious skull that transmitted oracles and supposedly dictated the so-called Secret Rule containing the most unimaginable blasphemies.

This legend is evidently the fruit of the imagination of 19th-century Romantic writers, because there is no earlier proof of the existence of a satanic skull.

The word Baphomet itself did not exist in medieval vocabulary; the Church and the Templars did not know it. It was invented by Occitan troubadours who used it on very rare occasions in their poetic confabulations. Although the Templars may have had a skull relic (they were great collectors of sacred relics), it would not have had this meaning. Even if, for Catholicism, it principally represents death, the skull has a double meaning. As it holds the brain, it holds the highest and greatest part of man. It is thus the quintessentially sacred part of the body and the symbol of the discovery of Supreme Knowledge. The word Baphomet comes from the Arabic phrase *ouba-al-fometh*, meaning the 'mouth of the Father', and in this sense is linked to the supreme knowledge that comes from the Father himself. As the Father contains the Son and the Holy Spirit, he is also the Light of Wisdom to which some gave the meaning, from late Greek, of *Baphêtmétous*. This is the meaning used in the poem *Ira et Dolor*, written in 1265 by an Occitan troubadour: '... *Baphomet obra de son poder*' ('And Baphomet made his power shine'). In the Moorish language of the Iberian Peninsula, inherited from the Muslims, it was written as *Abufihamat* (pronounced *Buphimat*) and signified 'Father, Source, Understanding'. An expression derived from it, *Ras-el-fahmat*, means 'Head of Knowledge' and refers to the mental capacity of a man who had reached a level of perfection of his conscience. This process is alluded to in the expression 'I'm constructing a head', used by some Sufic schools of the Iberian Peninsula. The medieval Christians pejoratively called it *Bafometarias* and *Carvoarias* (coal-like), meaning 'black and diabolical' in a popular sense. Indeed, secret knowledge was taught and practised in this tradition, which, for an ignorant Christian, could only be 'things of the Devil'. The 'baphometic' skull thus represents a mental illumination, just like Brigit the Celt when she presided over the pagan festival of Imbolc, a feast of purification celebrating the end of winter, a symbol of the illumination of the world after the infertile darkness. That is why Saint Brigid is also sometimes represented carrying a candle with a cow at her feet, signifying lactation, in this case a reference to the renewal of life in spring.

The Knights Templar: myth and reality

The Order of the Poor Knights of Christ and of the Temple of Solomon (*Pauperes Commilitiones Christi Temlpoque Salomonici*) – more commonly known as the Order of the Templars or the Order of the Temple – was the most famous religious-military Order of the Middle Ages. Founded on returning from the First Crusade (1096) with the declared purpose of protecting Christian pilgrims to the Holy Land, the Order would exist for more than two centuries. Officially recognised by Pope Honorius II in January 1128, the Order of the Temple quickly became the most highly regarded charitable order in Christendom, growing rapidly in both numbers and power. Distinguished by a white robe (revealing that members followed the Cistercian Rule of Cluny) bearing a red cross pattée, they formed the elite fighting force of the Crusades. The non-combatant members of the Order ran a vast financial empire extending throughout Christendom (even inventing the letter of credit, which was the first step towards the modern banking system). Ultimately, the Knights Templar had forts and churches throughout Europe and the Holy Land. This magnificent organisational structure had a double goal: the formation of what would today be called a United States of Europe, and the provision of free and obligatory education (in keeping with the principles of the Templars themselves). Thus, the Order became established at two levels: one was outwardly visible to the whole world; the other was a more inward, esoteric existence. The 'secular' arm, as it were, comprised dynamic men of action and soldiers, while the esoteric arm was made up of the Order's true elite: the wise men and priests who formed the 'rearguard' to a body of knights and warriors. The two groups answered solely to the Grand Master of the Order and not to any king or pope. It was this which led to them being suspected of heresy, even if all they were doing was observing a rule of obedience. Similarly, the secrecy surrounding the Templars' ceremonies caused people to imagine that they engaged in heretic worship – something which was never proved because 'civilians never enter into the houses of the military'. The Order adhered rigorously to Apostolic Catholicism, even if some of its members had an intellectual interest in other cultures and theologies, and Gnosticism in particular. Gnostic symbols are sometimes to be found in the churches and castles the Templars built. The spiritual mentor of the Order, Saint Bernard of Clairvaux, had initially selected nine members of its elite to go to Jerusalem, where King Baldwin III would allow them to establish their premises in the underground stables beneath the ruins of the Temple of Solomon. Certain traditions have it that they supposedly discovered the Cup of Solomon there, which had been hidden or lost since the time of Jesus Christ. The Templars are believed to have brought this Grail to the West, which from that point onwards extended its dominion over the whole world, just as the Order itself grew to dazzling heights. With the loss of the Holy Land, the support the Templars enjoyed from Europe's monarchs began to wane. The French king, Philippe IV, who had no way of paying off a substantial debt to the Order, would begin to put pressure on Pope Clement V to take measures against the Templars. Evidence was forged and rumours spread, both with regard to sexual practices and religious unorthodoxy. It was said, for example, that the Templars worshipped a bizarre demonic figure called Baphomet, of which little was ever known exactly – except that it was a figure of pure invention (see p. 217). Finally, in 1307, a large number of Templars in France were arrested and tortured until they made false confessions. They were then burnt at the stake or sentenced to service on the galleys. Philippe IV continued to pressure Pope Clement V, who finally dissolved the Order on 22 March 1312. In Portugal, however, the king, Dom Dinis, considered the Templars to be innocent and afforded immediate protection to the sizeable number who had fled there from France. After the dissolution of the Order, the king immediately founded another that incorporated the old Templars: the Military Order of the Knights of Christ, also known as the Order of Christ. The abrupt disappearance of most of the 'infrastructure' created in Europe by the Order of the Temple would give rise to a number of more or less extravagant legends and suppositions.

MACHADA GROTTO

A rainbow in a miraculous grotto

Igreja de Nossa Senhora da Luz
Largo da Luz, Carnide
Visits to the grotto on request at the church office (10am–2pm and 3pm–6pm)
Mass at 9am and 6pm
Metro Colégio Militar

Around 1437 or 1459, Pêro Martins, a Christian Templar knight, was being held prisoner by the Moors in Tangiers when Our Lady, infused with light, appeared to him. She promised he would soon be freed if, upon his release, he went to a place called Carnide in Lisbon and, at the spot where he would find her image in a grotto, built a chapel in her honour.

So it came to pass. Pêro Martins, once freed, quickly began looking for the statue at the spot indicated by the Virgin and finally found it in a grotto from which emanated a radiant rainbow-like light. He named the site *Luz* (Light). From this cave flowed miraculous waters that poured into the Fonte do Machado or da Machada, mentioned in a document dated 27 May 1311, and which was named after the woman who was the beneficiary of Chelas, Urraca Martins Machado or Machada, a Cistercian nun of the São Bernardo monastery in Carnide.

The church of Nossa Senhora da Luz (Our Lady of the Light), to which the miraculous fountain and grotto were annexed, was thus inaugurated on 8 September 1464 for the celebration of the Nativity of the Virgin, one year after the statue was discovered. The altar stands directly over the fountain of holy water, as the church is built over the little cave.

To enter the grotto of Machada, which can be visited by request, you pass through the Manueline gate of the first chapel, which was a site of pilgrimage. Then the gallery opens to where water flows into a sunken basin under an arch, above which is the statue of the Virgin of the Light, the Holy Child at her bosom.

Inside the church, the central painting of the surprising altarpiece by Francisco Venegas (17th century) depicts the *Alegoria da Imaculada Conceiçao* (Allegory of the Immaculate Conception), one of the rare female nudes (a Venus) to have survived the Counter-Reformation.

THE GARDEN OF THE CITY MUSEUM

The imaginery garden of Bordalo Pinheiro

Campo Grande – Metro Campo Grande
Tuesday to Sunday 10am–1pm and 2pm–6pm; closed Monday and public holidays

Boasting 1,205 pieces created by Rafael Augusto Prostes Bordalo Pinheiro (1846–1905), famous ceramist, decorator, designer and cartoonist, the garden of the City Museum (*Museu da Cidade*) has now been transformed into a ceramic zoo with snakes, lizards, giant snails, enormous wasps, giant lobsters, monkeys hanging from trees, etc. The garden is not to be missed. It was the journalist and businesswoman Catarina Portas who had the idea of creating a garden with original works by the famous ceramist. The project was implemented by the artist Joana Vasconcelos using giant moulds that had been stored for years by the Caldas da Rainha earthenware factory, which was threatened with closure. Carefully restored since January 2010, the pieces, which come from the brilliant imagination of this unique, prominent figure within Portuguese culture during the second half of the 20th century, are now on view. The project also includes azulejos that are representative of Bordalo Pinheiro's work, as well as bowls and large urns on pedestals. Among the wasps, frogs, lizards, cats, seahorses, tree trunks and magical mushrooms distributed around the garden's labyrinthine pathways, emerging from lakes or bushes, the most surprising elements in the collection can be seen climbing up the walls of the former Pimenta Palace, now transformed into the City Museum. Visitors strolling through the grounds are immediately transported to the fantastical world of the *Fables* of La Fontaine or *Alice in Wonderland*; adults and children of all ages experience the same fairy-tale world of the innocent imagination.

On seeing the ceramic sculpture *The Wolf and the Crane*, for example, visitors identify with the creative inspiration of the fable by Aesop, the Greek storyteller. This tells how a wolf choked on a bone that was stuck in his throat. In distress, he asked a passing crane for help. The bird came to his aid, slid its long beak into the wolf's throat and removed the bone. It then asked for a reward but the wolf refused, saying: 'You ungrateful thing. You should be thanking me for being able to put your beak into my mouth without being bitten, as I could have killed you! Consider yourself lucky.' The bird withdrew, regretting having helped the wolf. The moral of the fable: charity may not always be met with gratitude, and one can never expect gratitude from an enemy for doing them a favour.

THE EYES OF THE OWL
IN CIDADE UNIVERSITÁRIA
METRO STATION

A painter's humorous allusion

Corridor and ticket office of Cidade Universitária metro
Metro Cidade Universitária

On entering the ticket office of the Cidade Universitária metro station, one sees an owl with manganese and blue feathers, painted on the white tiled walls. The nocturnal bird of prey stares at passers-by with a slight squint. To its right, two dissociated human eyes, one inquisitive, the other watchful, sit playfully on the wall, evoking the upside-down world of cartoons.

The little owl with the bedraggled feathers and wild look is none other than the creation of Maria Helena Vieira da Silva (1908–1992), who, amused by the disturbing resemblance between her own sunken eyes and those of the night bird, displayed her own quite developed sense of self-depreciation by portraying herself in the guise of this animal.

Less prosaically, the prominent poet Sophia de Mello Breyner compares it to an antenna capturing and deciphering life in all its forms, in order to reveal its essence and legitimacy:

Vieira da Silva
Attentive antenna
Athens
With the owl eyes
Lucid in the dark night.

Painter, sculptor, ceramist and master glassmaker, Maria Helena Vieira da Silva lived for about sixty years in Paris, where she became a leading figure in the field of abstract landscape painting. She expressed her search for knowledge and the absolute through patchworks of lines with receding spaces and mosaics with an infinite variation of patterns. Libraries, mazes, cities and ports were her favourite recurring themes. By citing Athens, the gold standard for cultural openness in antiquity, her poet friend alludes to the artist who liked to see her works exhibited in transitory places (stations, the metro, and so on) in order to destroy the mystique of art. The owl, which symbolises knowledge and reason, could not have found a better location than that leading to the Lisbon university campus.

FUNDAÇÃO LEAL RIOS

Quality contemporary art in an as yet unknown space

R. Centro Cultural, 17-b
210 998 623
lealriosfoundation.com
Thursdays, Fridays and Saturdays, 2.30pm–6.30pm
Please enquire about workshop programmes with artists and lectures
Metro Alvalade

Unlike most Portuguese art collectors, who prefer to remain anonymous rather than entrust their large contemporary art collections to exhibitions, the two brothers Manuel (an economist who lived for a long time in Angola, born in 1963) and Miguel (a designer born in 1965) Leal Rios decided to create a foundation in 2002.

Thanks to them, the public can discover the different works in the collection, during temporary thematic exhibitions in the loft designed by architect Alexandre Marques Pereira and located between the airport and the famous Calouste Gulbenkian Foundation, on a former industrial site in the typical Alvalde district.

The collection reflects an interest in architecture, privileging the relationship between works and space, without neglecting videos. The brothers also personally know all the artists whose approximately 500 works are part of their collection.

The first acquisitions were devoted to Portuguese artists. Visitors can thus discover, among others, an important series of works by the great Portuguese conceptual artist Helena Almeida, but also by Lourdes Castro, Julião Sarmento ...

The collection has also progressively welcomed the works of international artists, such as Erwin Wurm, Matt Mullican, Cristina Iglesias, Lawrence Weiner ...

The Leal Rios brothers do not like isolated works, which is why they decided to bring together a collection of works that would allow the curious to discover the achievements of the artists in the collection.

As the space is limited and the days and times of visits are limited, visitors will certainly have the opportunity to meet the collectors or the curator of the exhibition.

TÁLIA THEATRE

A forgotten theatre

Estrada das Laranjeiras
Friday 9am–7pm, no appointment necessary
Metro Laranjeiras

Largely unknown, the Teatro Tália, now owned by the Ministry of Science, Technology and Higher Education, which uses it 'for scientific and cultural purposes', is near the zoo, in front of the former palace of Count Farrobo, built in 1820.

Originally a rather rudimentary theatre, it was reconstructed in 1842 with gas lighting, a grand innovation for the period. The premiere of Almeida Garrett's *Frei Luís de Sousa* was played here and 18 operas were performed between 1834 and 1853.

King Dom Fernando II and Queen Dona Maria II were frequent visitors. At the death of the queen, of whom the Count of Farrobo had been a great friend, the social and artistic life of the palace and theatre were put on hold. In 1856, theatrical activity began again with Italian operas and Portuguese and French comedies, but, on 9 September 1862, an accidental fire caused by worker negligence entirely destroyed the building. As the Count of Farrobo's fortune had started to dwindle, the theatre was not rebuilt and was left in ruins.

With an audience capacity of 560, the Tália had luxurious boxes and an opulent ballroom with walls covered in sumptuous Venetian mirrors that reflected the lights of numerous chandeliers, producing a dazzling effect.

It took around 150 years for the theatre to welcome spectators again. Converted in 2012 into a multi-purpose space, with an architectural project by Gonçalo Byrne, Patrícia Barbas and Diogo Lopes, the new Thalia kept the volumes of the foyer, audience and stage of the old Laranjeiras Theatre.

Thalia is one of the Greek Muses, the patron of comedy.

The theatre held a strong spiritual symbolism imparted by Joaquim Pedro de Quintela (1801-1869), second Baron of Quintela and first Count of Farrobo, who was a highly ranked Freemason. The building's exterior façade, reached by climbing four steps, is supported by four Tuscan columns fronted by the same number of Egyptian sphinxes. They symbolise the theatre of initiation entered into through the four-beat rhythm of the Earth (marked by the four seasons, the four phases of the Moon, etc.) and where everyone is the actor of their own evolution. At the top of the triangular pediment, a statue of Erato, the Muse of lyric poetry, holds her lyre in her right hand and rests it against her thigh.

SYMBOLS
OF THE PALÁCIO-MUSEU
MARQUESES DE FRONTEIRA

A hermetic garden

Largo de S. Domingos de Benfica, 1
Monday to Saturday, 10:30am–12pm

Now unfortunately surrounded by a desolate landscape of motorways and soulless buildings, the superb gardens of the Palácio-Museu Marqueses de Fronteira were designed in the 17th century according to hermetic principles (see p. 52) in order to attract the celestial energies whose principal elements it reproduces.

The Garden of Venus, which opens onto the Lake House facing a lake where a chimerical figure pours water into a basin, suggests the presence of a pavilion dedicated to mysterious ancient cults, as was the fashion in Mannerist gardens. These gardens reproduce the garden of the goddess of Love (Venus) on the former site of a labyrinth whose centre is now occupied by the lake. At the centre of the lake, an ancient sculpture of a young child bearing a coiled snake symbolises the Quest of and Initiation to the Divine Love of troubadours and minstrels.

The Varanda da Oratória (Loggia of the Oratory) is composed of niches holding statues of the gods of the Graeco-Roman pantheon representing the planets. The walls of the niches have azulejo panels depicting allegorical female figures symbolising the seven liberal Arts and their respective attributes. This sculptural ensemble is organised as follows:

Diana / Arithmetic – Mercury / Music – Venus / Dialectic – Apollo / Rhetoric – Mars / Poetry (replacing Geometry) – Jupiter / Astronomy – Saturn / Architecture.

The Jardim Grande (Grand Garden) is made up of a network of octagonal box-tree shrubs dividing four large flowerbeds which themselves are divided into four smaller ones. At the centre of the network lies a basin of water with a column surmounted by an armillary sphere. Four other smaller fountains and twelve lead statues (both masculine and feminine) stand at the corners of the flowerbeds. The low wall near the palace's east-facing facade is covered with polychrome azulejo panels on the themes of the four elements, the planets and the constellations, while the front wall

is covered with panels depicting the mythological allegories of the twelve months of the year and their corresponding agricultural activities. The north wall, opposite the central basin, bears azulejos on the theme of the twelve signs of the zodiac.

Structured in this manner, the Jardim Grande represents the Macrocosm or the Universe, in complementary opposition to the Microcosm, Man, symbolised by the Garden of Venus. The meeting point of the two is found in the Varanda da Oratória, where Science is assisted by the gods and where Hermes (or Mercury) emerges as the link between the general evolution of Man in the Universe and of the Universe influenced by Man, thus justifying the hermetic axiom according to which 'as it is above, so it is below' and vice-versa (see p. 52).

In the sublime Galeria dos Reis (Gallery of the Kings), the busts of twenty Portuguese monarchs are on display (the three Spanish kings of the Philippine dynasty who ruled Portugal during its occupation are absent) along with those of Count Dom Henrique (father of Afonso Henriques), Dom Fernando (the prince-saint, son of Dom João I, who died in captivity in Africa), and the Holy Constable Nuno Álvares Pereira. They stand along a façade of fourteen large blind arches, the centre of which leads to a grotto where Mount Helicon can be seen with the winged horse Pegasus and the eleven Muses, which recall the symbolism of the 'Isle of Love' evoked in the immortal Luís de Camões' *Lusiads*.

SYMBOLS OF THE ZOOLOGICAL GARDEN

Reproduction of the mythical Garden of Eden

Daily, 10am–8pm
Metro Jardim Zoológico

Considered one of the most beautiful gardens in the world, the Jardim Zoológico da Aclimataçado de Lisboa (Zoological Garden of Acclimatisation of Lisbon), inaugurated in 1905 at Quinta das Laranjeiras, Sete Rios, was originally an attempt to recreate the biblical Garden of Eden where humans and animals could coexist in peace. This zoo's project was apparently inspired by the Garden of Delights of biblical, Chaldean and Hindu accounts of paradise, where the four kingdoms of nature (mineral, vegetable, animal and human) come together in harmony. The mineral kingdom is represented by water and granite, the plant kingdom by the variety of flora, the animal kingdom by the zoological species presented, and the human kingdom by the visitors. The Freemasons and Rosicrucians that inspired the architecture of this exceptional site (the Count of Farrobo, Dom Fernando II and Dr António Carvalho Monteiro, among others) dispersed spiritual symbols throughout the garden to illustrate the different stages of the initiatory voyage. They thus recreated the Garden of the Gods in a recreational area that invites people to stroll and converse. Surrounded by hedges and pavilions at the heart of the garden, Lisbon's rose garden follows the style of French landscape artist Le Nôtre. A very pretty suspended bridge leads to the rose garden, an allegory of the passage to the superior world. At the top of each column of the bridge stands one of the four master Egyptian builders, the guardians of the four directions of the corners of the garden that, when regrouped in pairs, illustrate the Principle of Polarity that rules Universal Life (Spirit and Matter, Sun and Moon, Day and Night, North and South, etc.). The rose garden is like the garden of an open temple, with its fountains, hidden recesses, labyrinths, summits, granite spheres and wreaths, and mythological figures full of esoteric significance. The androgynous sphinxes (male face and female breasts) represent the perfect man, or the disciple that has reached his spiritual realisation. The Assyrian dragons illustrate the divine wisdom of the same disciple. The geese are an allusion to enlightened companionship and the dolphins a symbol of the philosopher's stone. The rose garden is planted in the centre of the cross of this enchanting, dream-like place and is a synthesis of the whole zoo.

The garden is also part of a spiritual path, or the 'initiatory voyage' of the human conscience with the goal of attaining eternal wisdom. The path includes several edifices of this former Quinta das Laranjeiras: the Farrobo palace (Physical); the Tália theatre (Vital); the Farrobo garden (Emotional); and the rose garden (Mental). Together, the Quinta represents Eden (Spiritual).

THE HEAD OF DIOGO ALVES

The head of this 19th-century Lisbon serial killer is kept in formaldehyde

Teatro anatomico della Facoltà di Medicina di Lisbona
Av. Prof. Egas Moniz
217 985 153
museu@fm.ul.pt
Visit by appointment at the office of the School of Medicine
Metro Cidade Universitária

Diogo Alves, a Galician born at Santa Xertrudes de Samos, in Lugo, came to live in Lisbon at a very young age. Nicknamed *Pancadas*, he quickly became famous as the Assassin of the Águas Livres Aqueduct. From 1836 to 1839, he committed a series of ghastly crimes there at the instigation of his girlfriend, Gertrudes Maria, nicknamed *Parreirinha* and who was the owner of a tavern in Palhavã. After robbing his victims, he would throw them off the top of the aqueduct (65 metres high) at night to simulate a suicide. The authorities finally captured him in 1840, after he and his gang killed a doctor and his family during a burglary. Curiously, they were condemned to death by hanging for this crime, but not for the aqueduct murders, which were not even mentioned in the trial.

He carried one secret to the grave – how he had obtained duplicate keys to the aqueduct galleries where he would lie in wait before attacking and assassinating his victims. It was not until after he was imprisoned and the apparent suicides ended that they were discovered to be the work of the sinister Diogo Alves, who killed 76 people in the summer of 1837 alone.

Once the death sentence had been carried out at the Cais do Tojo, at 2:15pm on 19 February 1841, scientists at the Lisbon School of Medicine and Surgery were so intrigued by his criminality that they retrieved his head for study. It can still be seen today in the anatomy theatre of the School of Medicine, preserved in formaldehyde. His calm expression provides no hint of the man he truly was.

The crimes of serial killer Diogo Alves, the last person to be condemned to death in Portugal in 1841, became the subject of one of the country's first silent films. His romanticised biography, which made his story famous, was first published in 1877 and reprinted in 2006. In 2005, his head was part of the exhibit *Cem peças para o museu de Medicina* (One hundred pieces for the Museum of Medicine), organised by the Museu Nacional de Arte Antiga.

Small businessmen and travelling merchants of the area frequently took the passeio dos Arcos (promenade of the Arches), the entrance of the public path to the aqueduto das Águas Livres (aqueduct of the Free Waters). It was closed in 1844, however, following the killings of Diogo Alves.

THE 'DIAPHANISED HAND' OF LISBON'S TEATRO ANATÓMICO

A veritable little museum of horrors

Teatro anatomico della Facoltà di Medicina di Lisbona - Av. Prof. Egas Moniz
217 985 153 – museu@fm.ul.pt
Visit by appointment at the office of the School of Medicine
Metro Cidade Universitária

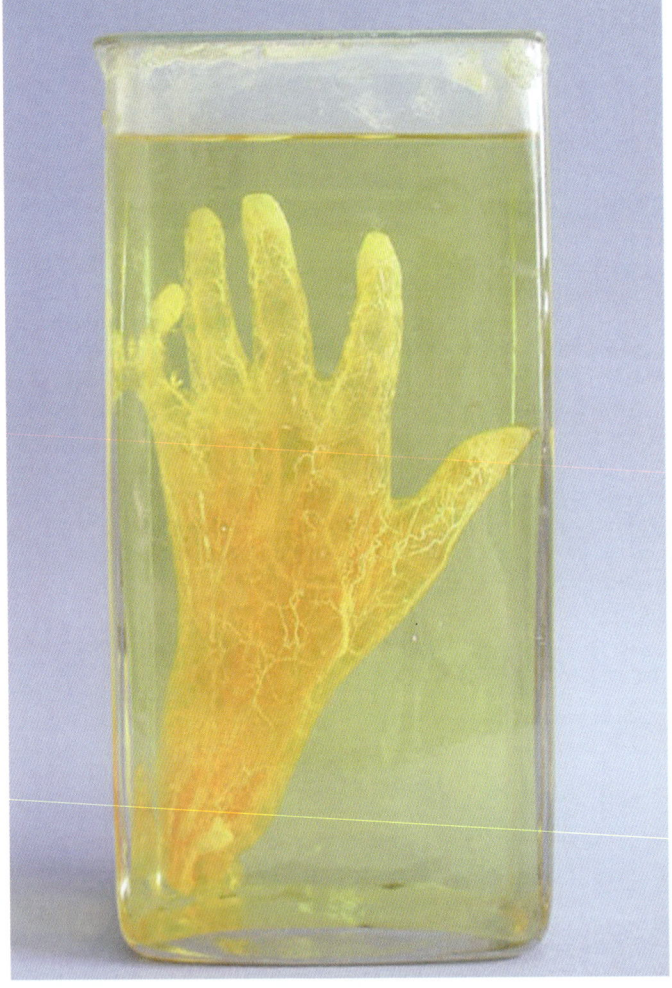

L isbon's anatomy theatre exhibits a series of human specimens that can truly shock more sensitive visitors.

This museum also possesses books and objects from the field of medico-legal surgery as well as a book dating from 1543 that the Lisbon School of Medicine inherited from the former School of Medicine and Surgery. Illustrated with detailed drawings of anatomical research and dissections, this book entitled *De humani corporis fabrica* by Andreas Vasalius (1514-1564) was for centuries the reference for medicine and anatomy in Portugal.

Besides all the teaching aids proposed by the museum, it also owns human organs preserved in various liquids, including the head of Diogo Alves preserved in formaldehyde (see p. 238).

One of the other spectacular pieces of the collection is a diaphanous hand, also preserved in a jar. The hand was made transparent, nearly invisible in fact, by a chemical injection that set, dehydrated and 'diaphanised' the tissues. The hand was then submerged in paraffin. In addition to the hand, there are dehydrated and coloured lungs, almost in fragments, revealing their bronchial tubes and bronchioles sub-divided and separated.

Typical artefacts of Portuguese medicine are also exhibited. Of particular note are several instruments invented and used by Portuguese professor Egas Moniz (1875-1955), winner of the Nobel Prize for Medicine in 1949, including an example of a syringe, a pair of *leucótomos*, and an apparatus for carrying out lobotomies and cutting the nerve fibres connecting the prefrontal cortex to the rest of the brain. Also to be found is the first cerebral angiography, a technique developed by Egas Moniz that consists of injecting a contrasting agent into the blood to see the blood vessels inside the skull by radiography, thus facilitating the diagnosis of cerebral pathologies, notably tumours.

Portugal's contribution to science does not stop there. There is the apparatus that Reinaldo dos Santos (1880-1970) used for the first aortography, a negatoscope and numerous other instruments that have made medical history in Portugal.

THE ANDALUZ FOUNTAIN BAS-RELIEF

The oldest example of Lisbon's coat of arms

Largo do Andaluz
Metro Picoas

On the Andaluz fountain, the discreet inscription dating from 1336 of a boat with two ravens, one on the prow and the other on the stern, is the oldest representation of the city of Lisbon's coat of arms.

The ravens are connected with the legend of Saint Vincent (São Vicente), according to which the birds watched over the saint's corpse as angels took it by boat from the coast of Sagres, in the Algarve, to Lisbon. He died in 1173, during the reign of Dom Afonso Henriques (see opposite).

Legend also says that the boat was a ship of the Knights Templar with black and white sails and that it carried the coffin to Lisbon Cathedral (Sé Patriarcal). As for the ravens, they stayed in the cloisters. A few decades ago, visitors could still see the birds flying around the cathedral, but today they are kept in a cage in a corner of São Jorge castle. The relics of São Vicente belong to the Sé treasure (see photo).

Symbolically, ravens are the birds that hold Divine Wisdom. They see the past and the future, like Huggin and Munnin (Thought and Memory) the companions of the Norse god Odin, who, perched on his

shoulders, caw secrets about the past and the future into his ear. The same goes for the two Hindu gods Kuvera and Mahima.

The lowered sails and ropes also form a six-pointed star composed of two interlaced triangles, the symbol of the universal equilibrium of soul and body.

The raven: the origin of the name 'Lisbon'?

The raven, a prophetic bird and messenger of the gods, totem of the Sun god Lug, was called Lu or Li in the Ligurian language (Genoese), which is the root of the name Lisboa or Lusibona, a derivative of Ulisibona and Ulisipa.

Saint Vincent, the saint of divine wisdom

Patron saint of Lisbon, Saint Vincent (São Vicente – Victorious One) is a Christian martyr from Valencia, Spain, where he was deacon. Martyred during the time of Roman emperor Diocletian (3rd century AD), he was burnt alive on a white-hot iron gate. According to legend, his corpse was then rolled up in ox-hide, attached to a millstone by the neck, and thrown into the sea. The tide took it all the way to the Algarve coast and deposited it on the cape that now bears his name, where a hermitage of Mozarabic Christians stood.

Some of the hermits noticed two enormous ravens flying around a corpse in the rocks. Upon closer inspection, they recognised the body of the martyr, which they immediately gathered up, with the birds looking on closely. The saint's remains provoked numerous

miracles and the site's saintly reputation increased to such an extent that it became nearly as famous as the Saint James of Compostela pilgrimage, which was rapidly developing at the time (8th century AD).

Later, King Afonso Henriques ordered that the saint's mortal remains be transported to Lisbon aboard a Templar ship. They let the tide guide the boat, still accompanied by the ravens, one at the stern and the other at the prow.

The symbols of Saint Vincent's sea voyage

There is a great difference between steering a boat and letting it drift. Vincent, who knew the secrets of this tricky maritime route, knew how to drift, meaning that he placed himself in the hands of Providence in whom he had total confidence. He thus illustrated the wisdom worthy of someone who had received the Holy Spirit. The detail that, according to legend, he came to Lisbon aboard a Templar ship, accompanied by symbolic ravens (see above), also attributes a special power to the Order of the Templars, thanks to their connection with the saint.

Finally, the millstone, the iconographic element of this saint, is in shape equivocal to a wheel. It is, however, impossible to move and turn without the very special Initiation that the force needed to accomplish this feat can provide.

PAVILHÃO CARLOS LOPES

A moving pavilion

Parque Eduardo VII
213 541 528
Visit by appointment
Metro Marquês de Pombal

Sited on the western fringes of Eduardo VII park, the former *Liberdade* (Freedom) park and green area of the city, the Pavilhão dos Desportos (Sports Pavilion) is one of the Portuguese pavilions of the grand 1922 World's Fair in Rio de Janeiro, organised to commemorate the 100th anniversary of Brazil's independence.

Built in Portugal by architects Guilherme and Carlos Rebello de Andrade and Alfredo Assunção Santos, the structure was inaugurated on 21 May 1923, nine months after the official opening of the event. During the fair, the president of the Republic of Brazil, Dr Artur Bernardes, visited the pavilion, where one of the many exhibits was the Santa Cruz hydroplane Gago Coutinho and Sacadura Cabral used to cross the Atlantic from Lisbon to Rio de Janeiro.

Rebuilt at its current location in the Portuguese capital by a renowned team supervised by architect Jorge Segurado, it became the Exhibition Hall and reopened for the large Portuguese Industrial Exhibition on 3 October 1932.

In 1946, the pavilion was renovated to host the 1947 Roller Hockey World Championships, which was when it became known as the Sports Pavilion. On 27 August 1984, it was renamed after one of the key figures of Portuguese athletics, Carlos Lopes. Note especially the stairs, the azulejo panels and the statues, particularly the two framing the main portico representing Science and Art, the work of sculptor Raul Xavier in 1935.

The four azulejo panels decorating the exterior façade at the front of the building date from 1922 and are by painter Jorge Colaço. They depict four great events in Portuguese history: *Ourique* – the battle of Baixo Alentejo that led to the foundation of Portugal, when Dom Afonso Henriques, encouraged by a vision of Christ, defeated the seven Moorish kings; *A Ala dos Namorados* (Regiment of the Lovers) – a unit of very young men (hence their name) commanded by the Saint Constable Nuno Álvares Pereira that won renown at the Battle of Aljubarrota and guaranteed the nation's independence; *Sagres* – the name of the Nautical School in the Algarve, as an allusion to Crown Prince Dom Henrique and the period of maritime expansion; *Cruzeiro do sul* – (Southern Cross, the characteristic constellation of the Southern Hemisphere that served as a guide for sailors), a reference to Brazil, discovered in 1500 by Pedro Álvares Cabral.

THE FEMALE FACES
OF THE HERON CASTILHO PALACE

Spectacular and impressive Art Nouveau sculptures

Rua Braamcamp, 40
Metro Marques de Pombal

On the corner of rua Castilho and the busy rua Braamcamp, the Heron Castilho building represents a curious mixture of styles, bringing together elements typical of the early and late 20th century, such as the stained glass windows that occupy the top four floors of the building.

Individually, many people fail to notice the huge and spectacular female faces sculpted under the first floor balconies on the facades of this corner building.

Built in 1921 by the architect Norte Júnior, the building that now occupies the first floors was constructed in an eclectic style, between Art Nouveau (with elements such as women's heads) and classicism.

On the corner of the two streets, a magnificent sculpture of a seated woman decorated the top of the building (see photo from 1960).

Unfortunately, the statue disappeared during a period of neglect, when the building was in danger of being almost completely destroyed. The building was reconstructed between 1985 and 1991, thanks to the design of architects Henrique Tavares Chicó, João Pedro Conceicão and Francisco Manuel Conceicão Silva.

SYMBOLS OF THE MARQUIS OF POMBAL STATUE

Pombal, the true leader of Lusitanian Freemasonry

Praça Marquês de Pombal
Metro Marquês de Pombal

The Masonic influence of the statue of Sebastião José de Carvalho e Mello, Marquis de Pombal, is openly illustrated even in the low grille that surrounds the statue. On its wrought-iron panels can be seen an interlaced sceptre and torch, allegories of various social activities that the marquis strongly influenced by reforming and developing them (agriculture, fishing, industry, etc.) in order to enter a new era of progress.

On the architecture panel, the architect's instruments are depicted in their symbolic Masonic use. Thus you can see the 'line of love' from which a triangle hangs. Attached to the triangle is a stonemason's hammer and, more importantly, the flaming torch of Knowledge intertwined with the sceptre of enlightened Absolutism that characterised the marquis's government.

It is unknown whether the Marquis of Pombal was actually a Freemason, despite evidence that he may have been initiated in a lodge in London or Vienna when he was the ambassador of Portugal in these cities. Whatever the case, he is the veritable leader of Lusitanian Freemasonry. Portuguese Freemasons paid him homage on his 100th and 200th anniversaries by transferring his ashes and building this monumental statue, financed by public subscription.

Dr Sebastião de Magalhães Lima (Rio de Janeiro 1850 – Lisbon 1928), a renowned Freemason and several times Grand Master of the Grand Orient Lusitano Unido, presided over the 1926 executive committee for the construction of this monument. Despite religious objections, this monument symbolising national unity under the aegis of a charismatic leader was finally accepted by the Republicans and by partisans of the New State.

Marquis of Pombal

Sebastião José de Carvalho e Mello, Marquis de Pombal and Count of Oeiras (Lisbon, 1699 – Leiria, 1782), held the position of Secretary of State (Prime Minister) of the kingdom of King Dom José I from 1750 to 1777. A representative of this enlightened despotism, he experienced Portuguese history of the Enlightenment at first hand and played an important role in bringing Portugal closer to the more advanced countries of Central and Northern Europe, notably on an economic and social level. In Portugal, he put an end to the auto-da-fé practices dating from the Holy Inquisition and to the segregation of New Christians (Jews forced to convert to Catholicism). He did not officially abolish the Portuguese Inquisition, however, which continued until 1821. He was also principally responsible for the expulsion of the Jesuits from Portugal and its colonies. His administration was marked by two famous difficulties. The challenge presented by the Lisbon earthquake of 1755 led to him being known in history books as the renovator of the city's architecture (according to hermetic principles – see p. 52). The Távoras trial was a political intrigue that had dramatic consequences. Although his affiliation to the Ancient and Accepted Scottish Rite of Freemasonry cannot be specifically proven, it is nevertheless generally accepted that he had close ties to the Casa Real dos Maçons da Lusitânia, particularly through Carlos Mardel and Reinaldo dos Santos, as well as to the Casa dos 24.

SECRETS OF CASA DOS 24

A 'Masonic' church in Lisbon

Igreja de S. José dos Carpinteiros
Rua de S. José, 64
218 855 230
Visit by reservation
Metro Restauradores

Less well-known today than it was during the Pombaline period, the church of São José dos Carpinteiros (Saint Joseph of the Carpenters) was originally called São José de Entre as Hortas (Saint Joseph among the Vegetable Gardens). In 1545, the Brothers of the Saint Joseph Patriarchate built a small chapel in the middle of the vegetable gardens that stretched north of the Santo Antão gates. It became a parish church in 1567. The church was the seat of the São José dos Carpinteiros brotherhood, which had originated in the corporation of the masters of the Casa dos 24 (House of 24) or da Mesa (of the Table). This corporation brought together the main trades of the city that gave their names to the streets of the Baixa district: *correeiros* (leather artisans), *sapateiros* (cobblers), *ourives* (silversmiths), among others. Founded during the reign of Dom João I (1357-1433) and abolished on 7 May 1834, the Casa dos 24 corporation met here from 1750. All the documents relating to its operation and spending, from the 18th century onwards, are still kept here, as are the brotherhood's original flag and the table they used for their meetings, which can be found in the chapel. This 17th-century table is made from tropical hardwood and has 24 drawers, one for each of its 24 seats. The São José dos Carpinteiros brotherhood, whose coat of arms (depicting the tree of paradise and the Freemason compass) is on the side door, began its activities in 1522 with masons and carpenters. Stonecutters, woodworkers and cabinet-makers joined later. Europe's oldest trade corporation, it probably inspired the speculative Freemasonry founded in France in 1717. The church facade was destroyed in the earthquake of 1755, but was immediately reconstructed under the orders of master-mason Caetano Tomás. On each side of the entrance topped with an oval Saint Joseph medallion, you can see carved stones on which the temple's important dates are inscribed as well as, in relief, masonry and carpentry tools, the philosophical significations of which are found in the names of neighbouring streets: Faith, Hope and Love (Charity).

The visionary and prophetic faith of these master tradesmen may have been identical to that of the discalced Augustine monks of Santo Antão o Velho who once had a convent here. Destroyed in the 1755 earthquake, it had become famous thanks to its abbot, Frei Maria da Visitação, who was condemned by the Inquisition for his controversial miracles and grandiose visions. However, these visions had brought him international renown, to the point that the duke of Medina Sidonia came to ask him to bless the standard of the Invincible Armada.

THE EX-VOTOS AROUND THE STATUE OF DOCTOR SOUSA MARTINS

16

The miraculous interventions of the 'Father of the Poor'

Campo Mártires da Pátria – Ascensor Lavra

The number of ex-votos piled around the statue of Dr José Tomás de Sousa Martins (Alhandra, 7 March 1843 – Alhandra, 18 August 1897), in the centre of campo dos Mártires da Pátria, illustrates the adulation still felt for him. He has almost acquired the status of a secular saint. Still today, the miraculous intervention of Dr Sousa Martins is invoked for health problems.

His statue, the work of sculptor Costa Motta, was inaugurated on 7 April 1904, on the initiative of a committee formed by the friends of the lamented professor. With this sculpture, Casimiro José de Lima was determined to keep alive the memory of Sousa Martins, head of the School of Medicine.

A tenured professor with degrees in pharmacy and medicine, Sousa Martins was most known for his intense, and often unpaid, work in the fight against tuberculosis. Not in the least religious and a strong humanist, he was a brilliant speaker gifted with humour and intelligence, a man who was always full of generosity towards the most disadvantaged. He had a great influence on his colleagues, students and patients, an influence that spread to such a point that people started coming to his statue, as well as his tomb at the Alhandra cemetery, to adulate him.

His fight against tuberculosis meant that he was exposed to the disease through his daily direct contact with his patients. Many died holding his hand and some even claimed to see a strange aura around his head. He often told his students, 'When you enter a hospital at night and you hear a sick patient moan, go to his bed and see what the poor patient needs, and if you don't have anything to give him, give him a smile.'

His skills as a clinician and his humanist habit of not charging the most disadvantaged patients earned him the title of 'Father of the Poor' as a sign of recognition from those he treated. This sentiment grew even more following the tragic circumstances of his death. He committed suicide after learning that he, too, had contracted tuberculosis.

He killed himself at dawn on 18 August 1897, leaving these words: 'Before snatching away a man's life, tuberculosis makes him endure a long martyrdom, and makes of the martyr an invalid.'

SOCIEDADE DE GEOGRAFIA DE LISBOA

17

A journey back in time

Rua Portas de Santo Antão, 100
213 425 401
Check the opening times on the website museu.socgeografialisboa.pt/visitas
Tours can be booked in other languages or on a particular theme
Metro Restauradores

Until work on the building is complete (date as yet unknown), when it should open more regularly, the Geographical Society of Lisbon offers guided tours once a month on reservation.

The tour, a journey back in time, begins in an old-fashioned salon with green velvet sofas before continuing up the central staircase.

On the first floor is an austere room with a large and elaborate ebony table, around which the institution's geographers, scientists, soldiers and other explorers used to gather.

The walls are hung with oil portraits of former society presidents, from the founder in 1875, Luciano Cordeiro, a naval officer with a special interest in Africa, to the current director Luís Aires Barros, who sometimes shows visitors around himself.

On the second floor, the most impressive sight is the 50-metre Portugal Room, with its furnishings upholstered in carmine and two floors of galleries where artefacts from various expeditions and the most important maps are kept.

The size of this museum gives an idea of the spirit of the 19th century, the international challenges faced by the European powers in their expansion throughout Asia and Africa, and the privileged position of Lisbon, the westernmost point of Europe, where 'the land ends and the sea begins', in the words of the great national poet, Luís de Camões.

Adjoining the Portugal Room is a small conference hall with a huge illuminated planisphere showing the routes of the Discoveries by Portuguese navigators, from Vasco da Gama to Gago Coutinho and Sacadura Cabral.

THE WAX MASKS IN THE MUSEUM ⑱ OF DERMATOLOGY

An impressive collection

Capuchos Hospital – Alameda Santo António dos Capuchos
218 170 593 or visitas.comentadas@cm-lisboa.pt
Visits at 3pm by appointment with the Lisbon City Department for Cultural
Communication and Publicity
Free entry

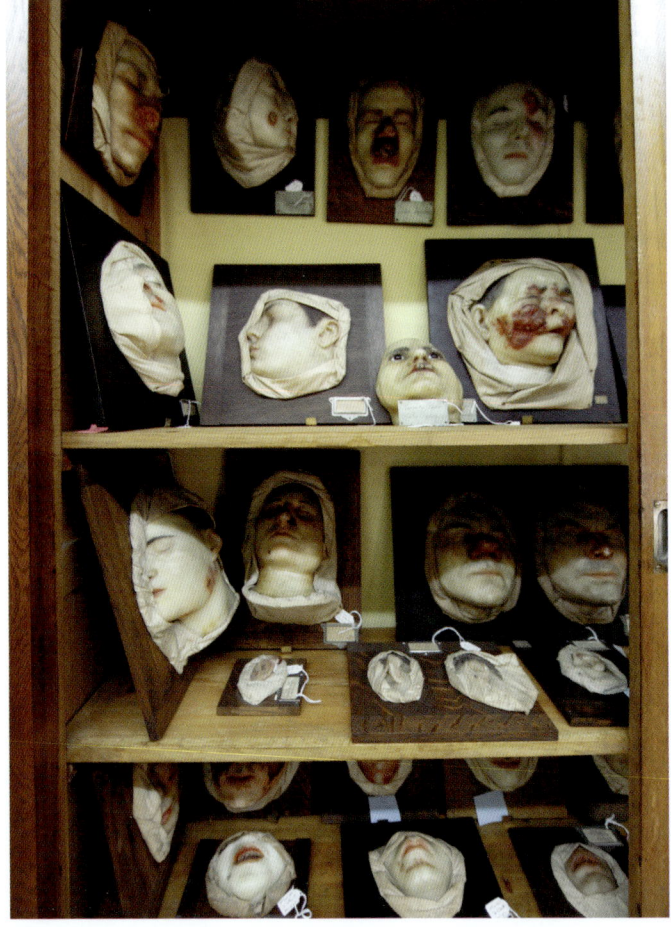

Situated inside the Capuchos Hospital, the Museum of Dermatology brings together a splendid collection of medical equipment, documents and photographs, as well as, most notably, a series of highly realistic wax figures portraying skin diseases. The collection includes 254 masks: 92 originate from the Dermatology Department of the Capuchos Hospital and were produced in fulfilment of an order placed by Dr. Caeiro Carrasco in the early 1950s, while the other 162 belonged to the Desterro Hospital (now closed) and were created for the Practitioner Sá Penella between 1930 and 1940.

These masks depict diseases that, thanks to medical progress, have either disappeared or are now extremely rare, such as syphilitic gumma, or advanced-stage Nicolas-Favre disease, certain forms of cutaneous tuberculosis or dermatological changes caused by the use of inorganic arsenic.

The masks were created by applying the moulds directly onto the patients. The body part being copied was covered in a non-adherent substance and a dressing. Once this had dried, it became the negative for the wound. A molten wax mixture was added, which then solidified. A positive wax version was thus produced and, to make it more realistic, it was decorated with individual, natural hairs and artificial eyes. It was then wrapped in cloth, mounted on a wooden stand and labelled with the name of the disease.

Unlike the exhibits in the famous *La Specola* (Museum of Zoology and Natural History) in Florence, the moulds came directly from patients suffering from cutaneous lesions – real people whose medical files were accessible.

The idea for the museum dates back to the 1940s, when the decision was taken to found three treatment centres for cutaneous diseases in the cities of Porto, Coimbra and Lisbon. In 1947, Caeiro Carrasco, director of the dermatology department at the Capuchos Hospital, proposed the creation of centres devoted to this specialism within all three units. In 1955, a space in the Desterro Hospital was allocated to what was then known as the Portuguese Museum of Dermatology. This institution had two objectives: to pay homage to the dermatologist Luís Alberto de Sá Penella and to preserve the wax figures depicting many of the diseases. In 2007, when the Desterro health facility closed, João Carlos Rodrigues, the learned protector of the museum's holdings, ensured that they were transferred to the *Salão Nobre* in the Capuchos Hospital. In 2009, the museum also received the Caeiro Carrasco collection.

THE LIZARD
OF PENHA DE FRANÇA

A lizard that saved the Lusitanians from paganism

Igreja de Nossa Senhora da Penha
Largo da Penha de França

Nossa Senhora da Penha de França church serves as an important witness of supernatural interventions in Lisbon. Indeed, a curious collection of ex-votos exhibited in a *casa dos milagres* (house of miracles) can be found inside.

Among all the legends surrounding this site, the main one is undoubtedly that of the *lizard of Penha*. A first version tells of a tired pilgrim who was sleeping on the slope of the hill as an enormous lizard prepared to attack him. The pilgrim was awakened by Our Lady, who thus miraculously saved him. Another version says he was woken up by the lizard, who was sent by Our Lady to save him from a snake attack, the snake thus symbolising the ancient 'pagan' religion of the Arabs, and the lizard the dragon of the Christian Lusitanians. Until 1739, a large stuffed lizard was kept in this church and was later replaced by a wooden version that was lost in the earthquake of 1755. The second version of the legend finally prevailed and today visitors can still see a carved wooden lizard and snake on the doors to the sacristy. The legend of the lizard is also depicted on the azulejo panel on the rear facade of the church.

The founding of the current Nossa Senhora da Penha convent by the order of the discalced monks of Saint Augustine dates from the end of the 16th century. Before, António Simões, a gilder of Lisbon who followed Dom Sebastião on the Alcácer-Quibir expedition (the greatest military disaster in Portuguese history), had had a modest chapel built here. He had made the vow to have nine different images of Our Lady made if he were to return safe and sound. He kept his promise – the last image was called Nossa Senhora da Penha de França and was placed in the Vitória chapel. On a cold night in 1597, António Simões, who had not yet finished the chapel, raised the standard of Our Lady in front of the chapel. The painting then started to shine extraordinarily through the night. The news quickly spread and worship of the Virgin of Penha took root.

Legend says that it is in this steep place that Ulysses fell in love with the 'snake-goddess' Ofiússa.

The name *Penha de França* has been kept in memory of a French monk who supposedly discovered a statue of the Virgin hidden in a rock, near where the church now stands, sometime during the Arab occupation of the Iberian Peninsula when Christianity was dominated by Islam.

PANOPTIC PAVILION OF HOSPITAL MIGUEL BOMBARDA

Original architecture in the heart of the city

Rua Dr. Almeida Amaral, 1 (Campo Santa Ana)
largoresidencias.com/info/ ver
Metro Anjos, Picoas, Intendente

A stone's throw from Campo dos Mártires da Pátria, the first psychiatric hospital of its kind in Portugal (opened 1848) forms an enclave in the heart of the city.

Behind the imposing neoclassical 18th-century convent of Rilhafoles, now converted into a hospice, stands the dazzling white Pavilhão de Segurança (Security Pavilion, 1896).

The avant-garde contours of this building, like a circus ring without its big top, anticipate the industrial aesthetic of the 1930s. Through its circular profile and perfect symmetry, architect José Maria Nepomuceno

sought to symbolise reason and perfection.

A panoptic (all-seeing) tower, now demolished, a single point of entry and an overhanging anti-escape roof, 40 m in diameter, allowed for the efficient and discreet surveillance of the inmates in an orderly setting. The 'accursed pavilion' held up to 80 mental health patients, some of whom were a danger to society.

The building, then known as the Rilhafoles Hospital, was based on the ingenious clinical and social methodology of Dr Miguel Bombarda. This modern-thinking psychiatrist and surgeon was director of the establishment from 1892 while actively involved in the revolutionary cause to depose the monarchy and set up a Portuguese Republic (1910).

In accordance with his theories, the hospital was built with curved walls and the fittings had rounded edges to prevent injuries to patients. The open-air patio reduced the spread of contagious diseases and oxygenated the brain.

Recalling traditional Portuguese architecture, the walkway benches were designed to encourage appropriate behaviour. Finally, the garden and the many skylights made the place more welcoming than a traditional prison.

The former cells, treatment room and refectory now show a selection of the patients' 6,000 drawings, paintings, writings and poems. They illustrate Dr Bombarda's innovative methods, the forerunner of art therapy. Taken from a collection of 1,200 photographs, dozens of portraits show the physiognomic (facial features or expression) development of the inmates.

Displayed in old-fashioned cabinets, electroconvulsive therapy equipment, a straitjacket, a cranial perforator and a scarificator (bloodletting instrument) give a more primitive image of the practices of the time.

On 3 October 1910, Dr Bombarda was murdered by an insane patient while in his office, which can been seen through a half-open window, on the ground floor to the left, just beyond the entrance gate.

What is panoptic architecture?

The 'panopticon' was introduced into penitentiary design by the liberal British philosopher Jeremy Bentham (1748–1832). Prison cells were to be arranged around a central tower or guardhouse so that detainees were always under surveillance ...

Outside the Security Pavilion, the Dona Maria II Bath House – a harmonious combination of Romantic, neo-Gothic and neo-Renaissance styles – indicates the emergence of therapeutic baths for use in the treatment of mental illness. The queen opened the facility in 1853 before an extended royal visit to the hospital.

The Security Pavilion has inspired several documentaries about the ambience of this forbidden place. In *Jaime* (1974), António Reis portrays a schizophrenic patient who produced numerous incoherent writings and drawings during his thirty years of incarceration. Karize Kresteniuk's *A cor do silêncio* (*The Colour of Silence*, 2007) takes a close look at mute patients who paint. *O tenente* (*The Lieutenant*, 2010) by Rafael Martins revisits the assassination of Dr Miguel Bombarda.

CHURCH OF SÃO FÉLIX DE CHELAS

The place where Ulysses came looking for Achilles?

Largo de Chelas, Marvila
Visit by appointment. Contact the army archives on 218 391 600

Still largely unknown (visits by appointment only), the church and convent of São Félix de Chelas have a rich and fabulous history that goes back to the time of the Greek hero Ulysses and his travelling companion, Achilles, and extends through the Visigoth period. It held so many objects to be admired or talked about that it became known as the 'temple of marvels' and inspired the name Maravilha (Marvel), and also Marvila, which became the name of the neighbourhood. In an ambiance of miraculous legends, visitors can admire the relics of the church's 26 patron saints which in 1604 were placed in sculptures commissioned by Dona Luisa de Noronha, the convent's benefactor. They are exhibited on the altars of the church apse. There are also vestiges from the Roman occupation to be discovered, such as the famous *Sarcophagus of the Writers*, so-called because of the four muses (Thalia, Melpomene, Polyhymnia and Clio) who accompany the writer on the frieze. The Christian origin of the convent dates back to at least AD 665, when Recceswinth led the Visigoth monarchy. He supposedly received the relics of Saint Felix (tortured to death in Gerona in AD 30) by a boat that crossed the estuary that then covered the Chelas valley. In the 9th century, Afonso III of León took Lisbon from the Moors and gave the convent the relics of the martyrs Saint Adrian and his wife, Saint Natalia, that came from Galicia. In 1147, Dom Afonso Henriques rebuilt the edifice, had it consecrated again, and gave it to the Order of the Knights Templar, who became the beneficiaries of the entire Chelas valley and the eastern side of the city. In 1290, this religious building already belonged to the Order of Saint Augustine, which, up until 1219, maintained two reclusive communities here, one for men and one for women; only the female community survived. From 1757, archbishop Dom Miguel de Castro had the relics placed in chests donated by Dona Isabel Scota to the *Nascimento* (Birth) chapel, and placed below the entrance where mothers passed through with their sick babies to invoke the protection of the martyr saints, before then going to wash them in the water of a well located on the estuary's former quay. This former convent still has its Manueline gate, the atrium's polychrome azulejo panels, the cloister's fountain and benches with sloping backs, blue-and-white azulejo planters, and staircases covered in azulejos.

A temple of the vestal virgins dedicated to Thetis, queen of the *Nereids* (sea nymphs) or *Tágides* (Tagus nymphs), apparently stood at this same spot in the 7th century BC. According to legend, Ulysses came looking for Achilles who had taken refuge here, living dressed as a woman and probably participating in a sort of matriarchal initiation. *Achelas* and *Chelas* (which was also spelled Celhas during the reign of Dom João I) are supposedly derivatives of the name Achilles.

THE HERMETIC AZULEJOS
OF MADRE DE DEUS

Symbols of secrecy and silence

Museu nacional do Azulejo
Rua da Madre Deus, 4
Tuesday, 2pm–6pm, and Wednesday to Sunday, 10am–6pm

A series of highly significant azulejos panels decorates the walls of Madre de Deus (Mother of God) church. This eastern part of Lisbon, of Braço de Prata or Lunar, was mainly inhabited by religious women and even some who had attained spiritual realisation, as was the case of some beguines of this very church, which made this a school of the hermetic tradition.

At the entrance, one of the doors bears the inscription RER, acronym of the Latin *Regina Eleonor Refacit* (Founded by Queen Leonor). Alchemically, RER also signifies the philosopher's vase where chemical transformations and sublimations of natural elements are carried out. It takes on the meaning of *Regeneratio*, as in the pious life of the martyr Santa Auta, represented with her chest pierced by an arrow, and whose remains have rested in this convent in a mother-of-pearl coffin since 2 September 1517.

The azulejo panels inside the church illustrate aspects of the religious life, not of the Franciscans, as might be expected in this Franciscan church, but of the Fathers of the Desert, like Saint Anthony the Hermit. Indeed, these hermits held the secrets of spiritual realisation, which required them to be silent, as is depicted on the portrait of a monk who clearly holds his index finger to his mouth (the panel at the back to the left of the altar).

Another large azulejo square shows the life of study, worship and work of the Fathers of the Desert, an allusion to the *lege, ora et labora* of the philosophers who practiced mystical alchemy, the strictly interior form (transformation of the lunar spirit into a solar spirit).

The path of spiritual realisation is represented by a long, wide alley lined with trees along which two figures, the master and the disciple, walk. Another panel depicts a cedar of Lebanon, the sacred tree representing the Tree of Life at the centre of the garden of Paradise (where a kneeling monk at prayer is surrounded by animals), here guarded by a crocodile, a symbol of the perfect disciple, incarnated by Saint Anthony, and the pope kneeling or in a position of submission at his feet, in the same way in which Peter bowed before John.

THE NATIONAL CENTRE OF UNDERWATER ARCHAEOLOGY

Fascinating objects found at the bottom of rivers, lakes and oceans of Portugal

Rua da Manutenção, 5
Guided tours by the Lisbon City Council: visitas.comentadas@cm-lisboa.pt
219 926 800

By reservation only, it is possible to visit the little-known National Centre of Underwater Archaeology, founded in 1997, where some of the treasures unearthed from the bottom of Portugal's rivers, lakes and oceans are displayed in an old tobacco warehouse.

Here, more than 20,000 objects were studied and classified before being sent to archaeological museums, local exhibitions and sometimes to private foundations. This activity continues today. These objects are first immersed in tanks to consolidate their structure and prevent salt corrosion. Then they are dried inside two rooms, where they are studied and passed under a 3D scanner to be listed in the centre's catalogues. Patience is required, as the whole the whole process can take up to 10 years...

Inside the numerous tanks you can see ceramics, swords, ship bows or cannons found all over the country.

You can, for example, admire the lantern found in the wreckage of a Norwegian ship sunk in 1917 by a German submarine off Sagres or a sword fished out of the bed of the Arade river with its secrets yet to be discovered: scientists fear that cleaning the blade may cause it to deteriorate further. Conservationists think the sword dates back to the Middle Ages and are waiting to find, some day the remains of the Viking fleet defeated by the Muslims during the clashes for the conquest of the city of Silves.

In the largest room in the centre, tanks house a series of cannons and large shipwrecks, including some from the French sailing ship *Océan*, sunk by the British during the Battle of Lagos (1759). On the wall of this bright room, the atmosphere changes thanks to the work of urban artist Nuno Bordalo, known by the pseudonym Bordalo II, for his sculptures made from recycled materials.

The work in question is entitled *Lighted Jelly Fish* and was commissioned by the government during the country's presidency of the European Council. Exhibited at the Council's headquarters until June 2021, 80% of the work is made from objects found at the bottom of rivers or on beaches.

THE MARITIME STATIONS OF ALCANTARA AND ROCHA DO CONDE DE OBIDOS

Anyone who has not seen Lisbon has never seen anything beautiful

Doca Alcantara – R. Gen. Gomes Araújo 1 – portodelisboa.pt
Visits by appointment only: 213 611 025/026
Relacoes_Institucionais@portodelisboa.pt
Tram 15E, 18E

By submitting a written request (see directions above), you will be able to visit the beautiful maritime stations of Alcantara and da Rocha do Conde de Obidos, which, even today, continue to welcome passengers

when the new terminal in Alfama is sold out due to the increasing number of cruise ships visiting Lisbon. Built rather closely together in 1942 and 1945, the two maritime stations were commissioned by Salazar's Estado Novo to make Lisbon a 'port of Europe' and impress transatlantic passengers, who disembarked here instead of being chaotically transferred ashore on boats among the shipments of fish, fruit and coal being unloaded from frigate ships.

The project was entrusted to the architect Porfírio Pardal Monteiro, in charge of numerous commissions from Salazar's Ministry of Public Works and a pioneer of modern architecture in Portugal.

Of the three stations initially planned, the one in Cais do Sodré was never built due to lack of funds (the architect would nevertheless christen the railway station with this name). The frescoes were entrusted to the multifaceted artist Almana Negreiros, who had already worked with Pardal Monteiro on the stained-glass windows of the church of Fatima

and the headquarters of the newspaper *Diario de Noticias*. In Alcantara, Almada painted a first triptych illustrating the legend of the vessel *Catarina*, as well as the values of family, homeland and religion, pillars of Salazar's propaganda.

The second triptych, entitled *Who Hasn't Seen Lisbon, Has Never Seen Anything Beautiful*, depicts scenes taken from everyday life, in which some women can be seen carrying baskets of coal on their heads (women were in fact available as cheaper labour than men). Their hands and large feet are reminiscent of neo-modernism. The government and the architect were very disappointed with this second work and even hesitated to confirm Almada's commission for the second station.

For the station at Rocha do Conde de Obidos, Almada showed drafts of drawings depicting the foundation of Lisbon by Ulysses.

However, with the help of his wife, the Spanish Sarah Afonso, Almada went even further in his provocation in order to denounce the living conditions of his own people. The first triptych, to the right of the station atrium, depicts a humble scene set at the port: departing lovers, acrobats, fishermen, black women with baskets laden with fish on their heads. The cubist influence, with direct references to Picasso (a young girl in the crowd and the harlequin), is self-evident. On the other side, we find a scene illustrating the departure of an ocean liner bound for Brazil or the colonies.

The expressions on the faces are sad. Each of the two triptychs is imbued with symbols barely concealed in the details: eyes concealed in the wood of the gangways, pentacles and pyramids (characteristic symbols of Freemasonry also present in Alcantara and forbidden at the time), a dove trapped under the veil of the hat of a lady left on the quay... Outraged by these frescoes, the government wanted to destroy them, but the curator of the National Museum of Ancient Art, João Couto, took the artist's side a second time and managed to convince the authorities to preserve the work. Almada Negreiros, in an interview given in his old age, said that the fresco of the Rocha do Conde de Obidos station was the work he was most proud of and which most represented him.

CASA DA CERCA

A charming hidden museum

Rua da Cerca, 2800-050 Almada
212 724 950
m-almada.pt/portal/page/portal/CASA_CERCA
Tuesday to Sunday, 10am–6pm

Perched on the highest point of the cliff, in the historical centre of the city of Almada, on Lisbon's southern shore, the Casa da Cerca is a charming and unknown museum dedicated to contemporary art and especially to drawing in all its forms. Dating from the 18th century, this small mansion has retained some Baroque traces, with a small chapel covered in azulejos, shaded by an orange tree and a red wrought-iron sculpture. The museum also includes a research centre and a unique botanical garden: 'the artists' land'.

The fruit and vegetables grown here are not eaten, but used to create the colours or materials to be used by the artists living nearby. Thus, for example, papyrus and flax are used to make canvas or paper, while oil-rich herbs and flowers are used to make fixatives for paint. And it matters little if water lilies bloom in the waterways: it is mainly the roots and their black pigments that interest the keepers of this garden. Throughout the year, the museum offers workshops for adults and children inspired by the exhibitions and the garden, as well as specific drawing courses based on the season and the museum's annual theme.

In June, on St. Anthony's Day, the gardens are the scene of a grand party, with concerts, a small design market and culinary delights. From August to September, concerts are also held at dusk.

A terrace with a view

In the afternoon, sitting at one of the café tables at the far end of the garden, away from the hustle and bustle, you can also enjoy a splendid view of the city, in the shade of a large cypress tree.

Since you are already in the neighbourhood, don't forget to admire the most impressive Almada cinema facade, not far from the museum.

CHAPEL
OF SANTA MARGHERITA

A secret chapel of incredible charm

Arrabida
F297+X7, Setúbal
We do not recommend visiting this cave in bad weather as it floods easily

The road to the Arrabida Natural Park, 50 kilometres from Lisbon, is truly breathtaking, with the green of the mountains and the turquoise of the sea that run alongside it. Here, among the inlets, protected endemic plants and tranquil gulfs, the Atlantic takes on a Mediterranean feel, with the crystal-like reflections of the gently lapping waves.

Once you take the small road (forbidden to cars) that leads to Portinho de Arrabida, pay attention to the large white building on your left, the Casa do Caiot: just ahead of it begins a small path that seems to lead towards a private property. After a few metres of dirt road you will find the first steps (200 in all) of a narrow stone staircase, often overgrown with vegetation, that will lead you up to 50 metres below the rock. A small belvedere will allow you to admire the horizon and will guide you up a new staircase, this time steep and dark, to the secret cave,

20 metres below, where the chapel of St Margaret is located.

Here, among the stalactites and stalagmites, many legends surround the altar built in the late 17th and early 18th centuries. Two of the statues (probably stolen) represented Our Lady of the Conception and St Anthony, while the third portrayed St Margaret. The statue is now kept in the convent of Our Lady of Arrabida, perched on top of a hill. It is said that a secret tunnel connected the altar directly to the convent. Lulled by the sound of the waves, this place was known for the pagan and initiatory rites that took place there, connected with the cult of maternity and the reincarnation of souls. This legend would explain why Catholics would in turn dedicate the chapel to Margaret, the patron saint of pregnant women.

Although the chapel is not in very good condition, the personal objects, Hindu deities and representations of Yemanja (the goddess of the sea) syncretized with Catholic saints give the place an incomparable charm.

It was here that Manuel de Oliveira shot a scene in the 1995 film *The Mysteries of the Convent*, starring Catherine Deneuve and John Malkovich.

ALPHABETICAL INDEX

NOTES

Thomas Jonglez

It was September 1995 and Thomas Jonglez was in Peshawar, the northern Pakistani city 20 kilometres from the tribal zone he was to visit a few days later. It occurred to him that he should record the hidden aspects of his native city, Paris, which he knew so well. During his seven-month trip back home from Beijing, the countries he crossed took in Tibet (entering clandestinely, hidden under blankets in an overnight bus), Iran and Kurdistan. He never took a plane but travelled by boat, train or bus, hitchhiking, cycling, on horseback or on foot, reaching Paris just in time to celebrate Christmas with the family.

On his return, he spent two fantastic years wandering the streets of the capital to gather material for his first 'secret guide', written with a friend. For the next seven years he worked in the steel industry until the passion for discovery overtook him. He launched Jonglez Publishing in 2003 and moved to Venice three years later.

In 2013, in search of new adventures, the family left Venice and spent six months travelling to Brazil, via North Korea, Micronesia, the Solomon Islands, Easter Island, Peru and Bolivia.

After seven years in Rio de Janeiro, he now lives in Berlin with his wife and three children.

Jonglez Publishing produces a range of titles in nine languages, released in 40 countries.

PHOTOGRAPHY CREDITS

All photographs by **Paulo Andrade** except:

Rupert Eden: Symbols of the equestrian statue of King Dom José I, Panels of the Restoration, Symbols of the cell doors of hieronymite monks, Alchemy and the religious order of the middle ages and the Renaissance, Machada grotto, Garden of the City Museum.

Camille de la Rochère: Why does the El Rei fountain have six water outlets?, Secrets of Tabacaria Mónaco, Last vestiges of the Hospital Real de Todos os Santos, Panoramic view of Lisbon, Mouse of Rato square, Eyes of the owl in Cidade Universitária metro station, Panoptic pavilion of Hospital Miguel Bombarda.

Charlotte Valade: Vila Berta, Stars of Estrella d'Ouro, Távora Palace, Roman stelae at Pedras Negras, Nativity scene in the Basilica da Estrela, Facade of Casa do Visconde de Sacavém, Secrets of Casa dos 24, Ex-votos around the statue of Doctor Sousa Martins, Wax masks in the Museum of Dermatology, Church of São Félix de Chelas, Hermetic azulejos of Madre de Deus, Maritime stations of Alcantara and de Rocha do Conde de Obidos, Casa da Cerca.

Johan Ricou: German cemetery in Lisbon.

Fundacão Leal Rios: Fundacão Leal Rios.

TEXT CREDITS

Camille de la Rochère: Why does the El Rei fountain have six water outlets?, Secrets of Tabacaria Mónaco, Last vestiges of the Hospital Real de Todos os Santos, Panoramic view of Lisbon, Mouse of Rato square, Eyes of the owl in Cidade Universitária metro station, Panoptic pavilion of Hospital Miguel Bombarda.

Charlotte Valade: Nativity scene in the Basilica da Estrela, Facade of Casa do Visconde de Sacavém, Wax masks in the Museum of Dermatology, Maritime stations of Alcantara and de Rocha do Conde de Obidos, Casa da Cerca.

Johan Ricou: Vila Berta, Roman stelae at Pedras Negras, German cemetery in Lisbon.

Marc Pottier: Fundacão Leal Rios.

ACKNOWLEDGEMENTS

Biblioteca Nacional de Lisboa, Dr. Eneida Voss, Palácio Foz, Dr. Sofia Carvalho, Associação Amigos dos Castelos, Dr. João Aníbal Henriques, Empresa Turística Tow, Patriarcado de Lisboa, Ministério do Exército, Câmara Municipal de Lisboa, Torre do Tombo, Museu Nacional de Arte Antiga, Museu Nacional de Arqueologia, Dr. Paulo Pereira (author of 'Lugares Mágicos de Portugal', ex-president of IPPAR), Dr. Manuel J. Gandra (Mythical History of Portugal), Professor Josué Pinharanda Gomes (pioneer of Portuguese philosophy), Museu da Cidade, Museu da Água, Comunidade Teúrgica Portuguesa, Dr. Juan Garcia Atienza (Mythical History of Spain), Museu Maçónico Português, Geoffroy Moreno, Rui Pires, Pierre Frédéric Coustols, Laetitia Monfort, Fiori Tiziana.

Maps: **Franz Huber** – Layout: **Emmanuelle Willard Toulemonde** – English Translation: **Caroline Lawrence** – English Editing: **Jana Gough** – Proofreading: **Kimberly Bess** – Publishing: **Clémence Mathé**

© JONGLEZ 2025

Registration of copyright: January 2025 – Edition: 04

ISBN: 978-2-36195-617-2

Printed in Bulgaria by Dedrax